"Approach love and cooking with reckless abandon."
(attributed to the Dalai Lama -- maybe)

POTLUCK

by
CATHY RUNYON

Copyright 2008
Golden Apple Greetings
5066 Lake Michigan Drive
Allendale, Michigan 49401
cathyrunyon@altelco.net

ISBN No. 0-9774324-2-4

INGREDIENTS

Family Meals: Exploding the Myth
p. 4

Kitchen: the Appliance Warehouse
p. 12

The Secret Ingredient
p. 24

How to Eat Like a Child
p. 30

To Market, to Market
p. 38

Ahhh, la Carte!
p. 46

Pot-blessed
p. 63

Table grace
p. 72

"Connection Collection" Recipes
p. 73

Family Meals: Exploding the Myth

1
Removable feast

Eating together is definitely overrated.

Leading authorities on the family keep trying to promote happy food-chewing faces spaced evenly around a table as an indication of healthy family relationships. It's not true. Watching a child stick olives on the ends of his fingers or hearing her compare the casserole to a smart bomb hitting a supermarket does not inspire me to affirm love.

Of course, mealtimes should be a kind of in-home workshop where children learn the art of conversation, right? Do you want to discuss business? Someone will be playing typewriter with the corn on the cob. How about literature? A mammoth Gulliver will be gobbling whole broccoli-spear Lilliputian trees. How about art? There's mashed potato sculpture, always an inspiration. "Look, Ma! It's Mount St. Helen!" and the gravy goes rolling over the edge from the crater in the middle.

Naturally there are strict rules against negative remarks about the food, but the creative child can always get around these. For instance, there is Saying Grace. (After all, kids know you can say anything to God, and if others are listening, too bad.) The child says something like, "Thank you for the Kool-Aid, and help me not to barf on my plate when I have to eat the two slices of carrot Mom gave me. And help me to be thankful for the casserole even though it has lots of stuff in it I really hate, especially sour cream that I asked Mom not to put in but she did anyway, and don't let Dad get a big spoonful when he gives me some to try because I know I'll just gag."

It's always at mealtimes that stories about the day's activities are related – things like a progress report on the level of decomposition of the road kill in front of Johnny's house, or a viewing of the shredded and only partially scabbed-over elbow which resulted from the fall off the bike, or the account of how someone at the park swimming pool swallowed too much chlorinated water and threw up – in the pool – after eating three chili dogs with onions.

Family mealtime, however has one real advantage that most people overlook. It's a great way to get a little time alone. For approximately 98 minutes before a scheduled meal, people will wander through the kitchen asking, "How long 'til we eat?" at intervals of 11 seconds. Sometimes they even come in groups of two or three to stand in the middle of the kitchen floor and supervise. Then, five minutes before the food is set to go on the table, the cook calls, "Dinner is ready," and suddenly there's not a single person in the place.

It's a learned response. You don't even have to be cooking anything to make it work. When I want some time to myself, all I have to do is yell, "Come to the table!" and everyone disappears. If we ever have a fire, I won't yell "Fire!" I'll yell, "Dinner!" They already know the shortest route out of the house.

2
Put it on the calendar

I was watching one of those public information television commercials that featured a good-looking young man standing by a dinette set while he delivered his message.

"This is something that can improve your family life," he said, gesturing toward the table.

My son happened to be in the room when I was watching, but he didn't seem interested in the actor's message. He wandered into the kitchen and migrated between the microwave and the refrigerator (he was looking at a 20-minute wait until supper) while keeping an ear open for the television programming change.

The actor urged families to employ this simple practice – gathering around the table on a regular basis for meals – to make their lives more harmonious.

"What do you think the message of that commercial is?" I asked my son.

"Easy," he said, munching stale popcorn. "We'd be happier if we ate more often."

Not long ago I told everyone in the family, one person at a time, to clear their calendars and plan on having a Sunday dinner together. On the appointed day my men left the paper, the television and the radio to come to the table after only the second call, and we actually sat down together for a meal. Approximately 12.5 minutes later, the meal was over and I was sitting alone with the leftovers. Still the goal had been accomplished. We had, for a few minutes, been together in one location, enjoying a home-cooked dinner.

It wasn't always this way, of course. We used to eat at least two meals together at the table every day, opening lines of communication by spilling milk into one another's laps. We had rousing debates on whether pimento is automatically hot because it's red, and light discussion on topics like who knocked the hairbrush into the toilet and why we can't keep a reptile in the house and the importance to the environment of the frugal use of Band-Aids.

Then we got older.

Part-time jobs descended on us. Ever-hungry teen-age friends began to wander in and out, collecting food on the way like black pants gather lint. Athletic practice schedules accumulated on the refrigerator door, and night-time college classes beckoned. Meals took on the appearance of a wilderness camping trip or a skid-row soup kitchen, centering on a single main dish simmering all day in a large pot. A stack of paper plates stood next to it with a 3-by-5 inch card bearing the hand-lettered message reminiscent of a 12-step program: "Help yourself."

For a while, I made it my goal to sit down at the table with anyone who was eating. I don't know if communication lines were kept open, but I gained 37 pounds.

Eventually, the kids will grow up, my husband and I will retire, and we will eat our meals all together once again – at Thanksgiving and Christmas when the grandchildren arrive. My feeling now, however, is that things will get worse before they get better. The youngest, who doesn't like regular food anyway, is about to enter high school.

Meanwhile, we've found another method for improving family relationships. Periodically we gather around the calendar to see if anyone is free to take the car into the repair shop.

3
Bring a plate – and shovel

The following is an actual inventory of the items found on a given morning on our dining room table:
- a classic car calendar
- orthodontic headgear
- a squirt gun (pump style)
- butter (in a dish)
- an original drawing
- an electric pencil sharpener
- a large paint brush with cardboard cover
- an electrical plug (no cord)
- a ninety-degree pipe elbow
- a used tissue
- a folded paper containing "The Bob family of spiders," tiny, whimsical arachnids made out of paper and the tassels from someone's loafers and named during a class period that must not have been too inspiring
- a 6 rpm motor switch
- pencils
- an exterior electrical outlet
- a nameless hunk of metal shaped like a ruler with holes punched in both ends
- miscellaneous bits of homework, including spelling and penmanship papers
- history and biology textbooks

Surely, you say, this must be an aberration. Someone was cleaning out a closet and got interrupted, perhaps by an air raid, before the job was through. Maybe a hurricane warning came before an ongoing insurance inventory was completed. Maybe the hurricane actually hit.

No, the truth is, this is not an extreme situation. In fact, on that morning I could still see parts of the table.

For some reason, the dining room table draws everything and everyone. We have five people in the house. Each one has a desk, yet most of the work seems to be done at the table, right in the middle of everything. (Desks are reserved for storing matchbox car collections, sports equipment, odd socks, Halloween candy, school carnival trinkets and so on.)

Occasionally, we also like to eat at the dining room table, which causes a problem. "Empty the table" is spoken as often as "Wash your hands" and "Come and eat."

Occasionally, I think I'll get tough and charge a fine for every item on the table that doesn't belong there – which would be all of them. So far, it hasn't worked. The accumulations gradually creep back. Besides, part of me enjoys having everyone busy in the middle of the house instead of all in their separate corners. Still, it would be nice to occasionally sit down at the table with only a spoon instead of a shovel.

4
Fresh batch of love

It was going to be his favorite breakfast – spicy hot sausage and made-from-scratch buttermilk pancakes, with boysenberry syrup.

You don't get a breakfast like that out of a box, so I started planning the night before. I shaped the sausage patties, covered them with waxed paper and put them in the refrigerator, ready to pop into the skillet. I mixed dry ingredients for the pancakes in one bowl, wet ingredients in another, ready to combine in the morning for almost-instant pancakes. I even got out the syrup and put it on the table before I went to bed.

In the morning, however, we were running a few minutes late. I decided to cook the sausage in the microwave but couldn't remember just how long it took to cook that many patties. I put them in for one minute, then turned them and cooked them for another minute. They looked all right.

I mixed up the pancake batter, having already turned on the griddle. Still, there was no satisfying sizzle when the batter hit the hot surface, and I knew in my heart the pancakes would be pale and a little dry.

Seeing half the sausage remaining on his plate, I asked my husband if it was all right, and he said it was a little rubbery, but never mind, that was OK. He thanked me heartily for the breakfast and went to work.

While I was clearing the table, I noticed the pancakes seemed a little thinner than usual and took a bite of one he had left on his plate. Sure enough, instead of self-rising flour I had used all-purpose flour. The pancakes were as flat as – well, as flat as pancakes and as tasteless as wallpaper paste. Only the syrup made them palatable.

As disasters go, this one was pretty mild. It was the everyday variety – a hope that wasn't realized, a plan that fell through, something that could have been a bright point in a dull day and instead, was best forgotten. There are lots of mild disasters. They are caused by our own failures, or by the carelessness, indifference, or malice of others.

So I threw the leftover pancakes into the garbage, rinsed the plate and that was that. No amount of analysis or penance or resolve would make that breakfast right. It was over. I gave thanks for a husband who loves me in spite of bad meals and I started thinking about lunch.

There are a lot of moms and dads who go to bed each night scheming to set the past right and make tomorrow perfect. In their minds, they hold the baby more (or maybe less); read to their toddlers instead of letting them watch television; are not so tired at the end of the day to say yes when their children want to play catch, make cookies or back the car out of the garage. They can see it happening the way they wanted it to happen, with grace and patience instead of argument and disappointment.

It's time to throw out the garbage and rinse off the residue. The hopes and dreams we all have for our families are glorious when they appear, but when they don't, take the ingredients you have at hand and start over, beginning where you are.

We go on eating day in and day out until the end of our lives, continually generating and using up resources. Should loving be any different?

Kitchen: the Appliance Warehouse

1
Got you covered

Most family histories are not in memory books but on the door of the refrigerator. The other day I decided it was time to update my family's files and began pulling off the magnets and shuffling through the sheets of paper and prying apart the sticky notes, the edges yellowed with age and cheese curl coating.

My husband wandered in. "Is this the week we put out the recyclables?" he asked, looking at the mounds of paper on the floor.

"No, I'm just updating the refrigerator. Besides, it would be fun to find out what color it is."

"You don't want to throw this away, do you?" he asked, fishing a sheet of canary yellow paper from the pile. "It's the school lunch menu."

I pointed to the date, October 1996. "I think we can manage without it," I said. Still there was a moment of panic as I dumped it in the trash. What if we needed it next week?

He said, "Here's a note that says, 'Don't eat the banana pudding. It's for the picnic.' Are we having a picnic?"

"We had one five months ago but somebody ate the banana pudding before the picnic anyway. The note was covered up by the dentist's appointment card. We missed the appointment because that was covered by the notice to renew the license plates. It's called prioritizing."

There were soccer practice schedules from seasons past, school newsletters, church party notices, grocery lists on the backs of envelopes, recipes clipped from cereal boxes, coupons, missionary prayer letters, teachers' notes, field trip permission slips, an electric bill that read "final notice" in big red letters, a baby shower announcement and a report card with a sad face sketched in.

A few years ago I began studying people's refrigerators and noticing how product marketers took advantage of the phenomenon of front-door accumulation. Somebody came out with a magnetic alphabet so preschoolers could use the door as an educational play surface. Another company, one-upmanship-fashion, came out with a magnetic refrigerator door.

Magnets are the way to go. Refrigerator magnets have become a kind of pop art expressing everything from theology to the current diet hysteria, a true representation of our society and a study in classic one-liners ("You're not fat, you're fluffy."). I wonder if further study will reveal that the real reason for being overweight or undernourished is that magnets are sucking all the vitamins right through the refrigerator's front door.

Somehow the refrigerator seems like the perfect place for hand-drawn maps to Jennifer's house, old church bulletins with the airplane folds still showing, emergency calling lists, menus on which someone has written "YUK" in blueberry-scented felt marker, jam-covered post cards from a friend on vacation, photos and homework and business cards.

Refrigerators get bigger and bigger, not because people have more food but because they have a lot more paper.

2
Why couldn't there be global cooling?

There is a beast that lurks in inaccessible corners of homes throughout this land. It hums in sinister tones while hoarding within its icy heart the best efforts of careful mothers and the humble offerings of children. It's the family freezer, and believe me, it isn't as innocent as it might appear.

Of course, the chest freezer's real purpose is to provide yet another flat surface where gloves, spare bike parts, school books, scrap lumber, broken toys and gardening paraphernalia can accumulate. If you are fortunate enough to get anything into a chest freezer, you will probably never be able to get it out. If it's in the basement or, worse yet, in the garage, as mine is, your chances of ever opening the lid approach those of a single woman marrying after the age of 40.

Not that it does much good for me to open the lid. Once inside the freezer, packages shift about at will and the ink on the labels runs to form a dark, unreadable blob. After all, it's dark in there and no one is really in charge. I can carefully stack all the beef roasts in one basket and when I get one out to thaw, it turns out to be leftover Thanksgiving stuffing. Where do the mischievous freezer gnomes go when it's time to defrost?

Don't think you are safe if you buy an upright freezer. You can't stack anything on top, but when you open the door and a six-pound pot roast falls out onto your foot, you'll wish you had the other style.

The first boy I dated when I went to college shared with me his greatest personal fear – that during his absence from home, his mother would throw away the wad of Juicy Fruit gum he had been storing in the freezer for nearly a year. Our relationship never matured.

My own children like to freeze gum and also glasses of pop, which they know beyond the shadow of a doubt will never crack or spill and all the cracked, spilled glasses of the past were mere aberrations. This time it will be different – they will be careful, and anyway, it's worth it for a spoonful of slush, especially when the outside temperature is minus 15 degrees and you have to wash the stuff down with hot chocolate. Frozen chocolate bars or caramels are good too, especially if you are trying to set a record for the most visits to the orthodontist in a single month.

Although billed as a great convenience, the freezer actually prevents me from accessing any food quickly. I can have a freezer full of food, but if I need something in a hurry, peanut butter is still my best option. Some people think the microwave was invented to cook food quickly. Actually, it never caught on until somebody promoted it as a thawing device.

I've developed a great system: I buy more than we can eat, wrap the excess in non-recyclable material, wrestle it into the freezer where it takes up space and energy until I forget it's there, and when I need something for dinner, I run out to the store and again buy more than we can eat. This is called convenience.

Of course, there are wonderfully organized people who keep a list taped to the top of the freezer beside a little map indicating the location of vegetables and meat, fruit and casseroles. Contributions to the freezer are carefully noted, extractions diligently crossed off. These people plan meals three days in advance so their meat can safely thaw in the refrigerator. If you looked in the attic at their homes, somewhere you would find a diploma indicating a college degree in freezer management.

I don't have a degree or even a certificate. I'm still trying to remember what kind of reasoning prompted me to freeze ten pounds of chicken thighs together in a lump. Oh, well. Next month, when they finally thaw, I'll invite the basketball team over for a cookout.

3
But what would you do without it?

When you begin preparations for Thanksgiving dinner, I hope you have one of those amazing turkey basters on hand.

In case you don't know what it is, the turkey baster is like a 10-inch-long hypodermic needle as big around as a clarinet. It has a rubber bulb on the end which you squeeze while inserting the hollow point into the turkey broth in the bottom of the roasting pan. Then you release the bulb, sucking the juice up into the tube. Then you squeeze the filled bulb to squirt the juice over the bird. No messy digging around with a spoon or ladle. It's one of the true wonders of the gadget industry.

A gadget is a lot like a tool, except tools cost more and usually a tool can be used for more than one thing. I came across a strawberry huller in the drawer I reserve for my gadget collection. For a minute, I couldn't remember what it was. It looks like a set of tiny tongs, or cheap tweezers with rounded ends. I bought it long ago in a frenzy of organizational fervor, convinced that good mothers had to make their own jam. It hasn't been used since that first summer.

My mother made jam every year, hulling dozens of quarts of berries using a paring knife, one of the world's great tools and not to be confused with gadgets.

Kitchens are full of appliances that do exactly one thing. Electric lettuce slicers, crepe makers, burger fryers, orange squeezers, nut choppers and potpourri crocks seem so logical when you give them or get them as gifts. Sometimes you even use them, but often as not they end up in the back of the silverware drawer or behind the saucepans, out of sight, out of mind.

How do those Mexican housewives get along without tortilla presses? How have the Chinese managed for thousands of years without electric rice steamers? For every cooking chore, there is a gadget, if only you look.

For a real adventure in gadget shopping, however, you must leave the department store and sit down with one of those novelty catalogs that come in the mail about this time of year. There you can find trays to make mermaid-shaped ice cubes, electric nose hair trimmers, sponge rolls to relieve pressure from too-tight hair dryer hoods, musical bathroom tissue holders and miniature clothespins to hang up Christmas cards.

In a world where much of the population still has survival as its daily goal, we have individual insulated beverage can coolers. In other countries, people wonder if they will eat tomorrow; we roast meat in disposable plastic oven bags so we won't have to wash the pan.

Gadgets are just one small indication of the prosperity with which we are blessed. "Bless this food and the hands that prepared it," is a common beginning to table grace. We might add, "and thank you, Lord, for such abundant gadgets," because only in a country as rich and free as ours do people have the time, energy and resources to create and market things like chip clips and corncob holders

4
Now THAT'S helpful!

We once had a car that talked to us. If you started to get out of the car and left the key behind, an authoritative voice stated, "The key is in the ignition."

I'm sure it thought it was being helpful, but really, that's a classic example of stating the obvious. If the car wanted to be genuinely helpful, it would tell me things I don't know. "The key is in the pocket of your navy blue jacket," or "The key is under the middle cushion of the couch."

Still, getting machines to talk is not a bad idea, and if extended to other devices around the house, could be very supportive. The bathroom could be made more vocal. Forget "Who's the fairest of them all?" The bathroom mirror should say, "The tag on your sweater is out," or "The mascara wand has rolled under the corner of the vanity," or "That lipstick is not in your color palette." A talking tissue holder wouldn't do any good if it only said, "The roll is empty." It would have to say something like, "If you don't replace the roll, I'll tell Mom you were the last one in here."

Something that would be really useful would be a talking refrigerator. It would be like a combination cook and nanny.

When someone keeps the door open too long, the refrigerator would not say, like the automobile, "The door is ajar." Anyone can see that just by reading the electric bill. The well-designed talking refrigerator would say, "What are you trying to do, cool off the whole world?" It could say, "Don't put the empty milk jug back inside," or "Don't complain. The children in Ethiopia would be glad to have what you're sneering at right this minute."

The kitchen just begs for interactive speech. A talking cookie jar ("Put a lid on it!"), a talking lunch box ("Homemade cookies are best.") a talking toaster ("Stop watching. It will pop up when it's done.") would all add interest to our lives.

I suppose the talking car is a social indicator – the failure of humans to communicate on a personal level, or to take responsibility for their possessions or decisions – but I think it's a smart idea, and it's time to take it from the garage to the house.

5
Just don't turn your back

There's only one thing worse than a toaster that doesn't pop up the toast, and that's a toaster that doesn't pop up the toast *sometimes*. Just when you begin to trust it, it betrays you.

Toasters weren't always automatic. I have memories of one that was shaped like the tents kids make with a blanket on the clothesline. I think it had been my grandmother's and dated back to the 1930s. The sides were like little trays, hinged at the bottom, on which a slice of bread was placed. When the side of the toaster was closed, the bread snuggled up to heating coils which toasted one side. After an appropriate time, we took the bread out, turned it over, and toasted the other side. We never went away to pour coffee or feed the canary while waiting for the toast to pop up. It didn't – ever – so we stood guard.

Unlike many newly married couples, my husband and I did not receive multiple toasters as wedding gifts. In fact, we didn't receive any. A friend of my mother's gave us an old one after she put a new cord on it. It was about 20 years old, as big and shiny as an Edsel, but unlike that car, absolutely dependable. We used it for years and years.

When Old Faithful stopped popping up, we went to a thrift store and got a used toaster for about $3. On the tag, it said only one side worked, so we didn't expect much from it. What the tag didn't say was that the other side worked *occasionally*.

After a couple years of burned bread, we took the plunge and bought our first new toaster, on sale for about $10. It worked beautifully for approximately 11 days, after which it became temperamental, apparently unhappy with its career choice. After a few months, it didn't pop up at all, and we were back in manual mode, just like Grandma enjoyed.

Trapped in the mechanistic lifestyle to which we had become accustomed, we never watched that toaster as diligently as we should have. Before long, the cost of burned bread would have paid for a new toaster. Unwilling to build a campfire and toast bread on a long fork every morning, we purchased another appliance – a better brand, higher-priced toaster that worked beautifully – most of the time. The toaster developed anxiety when entrusted with bagels and toaster pastries. Apparently it was happy on the assembly line, but didn't want to make the move to management.

It wasn't a bad toaster. It just had authority issues and functioned independently just often enough to keep us off our guard. You know the old saying. "Where there's smoke, there's a sometimes-automatic toaster."

6
Or you could build a fire

The cold snap put me in the mood for homemade vegetable soup, and I decided to make it right. I began by simmering beef shanks with onion and seasonings all day long.

It wasn't quite like the old days when Mom put the kettle on the back of the cookstove, but it was close. I used an electric slow cooker. By evening, the broth was ready. The next day I put in the rest of the vegetables and let them cook until supper time. It was perfect.

Of course, the great thing about homemade soup is that it's even better the second day. The funny thing was, the next day, when I wanted to have a bowl of it for lunch, I put it in the microwave. Soup that took two days to make was ready to eat in 50 seconds.

There are more ways to cook food than Imelda Marcos had shoes. Besides the slow cooker and the fast warmer-upper in my kitchen, there's the gas stove and oven, conveniences that carry the bulk of my cooking chores. There's an electric griddle that allows me to make eight grilled cheese sandwiches or pancakes at a single whack, and an electric skillet that is great for goulash. We have an electric grill and a gas grill, a toaster oven, and a coffee maker, which can double as a source of hot water for tea or instant hot chocolate.

In storage, just in case we need them, are two electric roasters, a rice cooker and a waffle maker.

I feel better about my materialism when I compare myself to others who have more. I don't have an individual hamburger or sandwich griller, deep fryer, fondue pot, hot dog cooker, rotisserie, potato roaster or vegetable steamer – yet.

With so many ways to cook food on any time schedule, why did we recently end up with take-out chicken and potato salad for dinner? It made me think of the story I heard about a woman who shopped at the grocery store on her way home from work and selected a four-minute microwave dinner for her evening meal, then had second thoughts and put it back in the frozen food bin. She decided to eat out because she was too tired to cook.

No matter how easy cooking is, there are some who want to make it hard. I read a story about a woman who coaxed her husband into building a fireplace in their home, and installing a hook so she could hang her chili pot over the fire Pilgrim-style. Even in my family, when we could stay home and eat ready-cooked food warmed without heat in the microwave, we sometimes truck a load of supplies to the park and burn our fingers while we cook meat on a stick held over a smoky fire.

Is all this extra effort for the flavor? Sometimes. More often it's the pattern of turning what was once a necessity into a hobby. Other examples of this trend are sewing, handwriting (now calligraphy), basket weaving, pottery making and horseback riding. At one time in history we had no choice about those activities; now we do them to keep in touch with our roots, as an expression of our artistic nature.

Cooking has become a leisure time activity complete with a marketing package that rivals Paris Hilton. Ethnic cooking classes, kitchen gadget home parties, specialty shops, cookbook clubs and catalogs and magazines by the score stand ready to help us cook. Entire television networks are dedicated to it. Web sites clog the networks offering recipes. Still we eat peanut butter sandwiches on store-bought bread.

We know a watched pot never boils, and too many cooks spoil the broth, but trust me, someone, somewhere, is at this moment patenting an automatic pot watcher and marketing instant broth mix suitable for multiple cooks. Those who buy them will probably use canned soup just the same.

7
More hazardous than smoking?

For the first time in my life, I've read the safety instructions for a household appliance. I wish I hadn't. I am now afraid to go into the kitchen for fear the stove we just got will attack me.

As soon as I started reading, I was glad I didn't live in California, and it has nothing to do with brush fires or earthquakes. There's a special warning in the book for people living in California informing them that burning gas for cooking can result in low-level exposure to things like benzene, formaldehyde, and soot. Maybe that's why they eat so many raw vegetables out there.

Of course, there was a suggestion that I write down the model number and serial number for future reference. Those numbers, I learned, could be found on the rating plate located on the sides of the lower range front frame. To see them, I should pull out the lower drawer and lay flat on the floor to find where they are printed in 4-point script on the underside of the stove frame. With a magnifying glass and flashlight in one hand, I should jot down both 22-digit numbers.

I wouldn't risk doing that, because in the very next column, there is a drawing of a kitchen range maliciously tipping over onto a man, driving him to his knees, while a pan of hot liquid falls from the stove to scald him. "Warning," it says, "all ranges can tip. Install anti-tip devices packed with range." I don't know what an anti-tip device is. I have never heard of a kitchen range tipping over without a lot of help, but it must happen or it wouldn't be in the book. To check if the device is already installed, the book said, use a flashlight and look underneath the range to see if one of the rear leveling legs is engaged in the bracket slot. No way! I'm not laying down in front of that stove for anything, even if I thought I could get back up again without help.

On page two, another drawing shows a modern housewife, complete with apron and high heels, falling backward from her precarious position on the oven door. She has made the near-fatal error of using the oven door as a step stool when the book clearly says, "Caution: Do not use an appliance as a step stool to cabinets above." Besides the danger of falling backward, it's possible that the anti-tipping device wasn't installed, and overloading the oven door could lead to tipping, breaking the door and serious injuries.

There were other dire situations described. Don't turn on the oven (once you learn how) when there is packing material still inside. (I'm so glad they told me.) Don't store gasoline in your kitchen near the stove, ditto aerosol cans. (I'm so relieved. I was planning to do that very thing.)Don't touch the stove when it's hot. Don't heat food on the stove in unopened cans. Don't let pans boil dry. Don't let children into the same room with this dangerous appliance, but if you do, teach them that the stove is not a toy and never, never let them use the oven door as a step stool (see paragraph above if you need the reasons why).

I did learn a few things, and I have decided to relocate my paper towel holder so the towels won't catch fire. Still, in the three pages of warnings – over 60 items – I kept getting the feeling it wasn't my safety that was the issue, but corporate liability. Now when the plastic bowl melts because I lit a flame under it, no one can say I wasn't told.

The Secret Ingredient

1

Stovetop chameleon

Some questions are just bound to get a discussion going, like what's the best way to burp a baby, at what age should teenagers date, and was O.J. guilty (pick a crime, any crime)?

My favorite is, "How do you make goulash?"

Like the color taupe, goulash has no definition in our society. The word is a corruption of the Hungarian "*gulays*," which simply means "soup." But it doesn't look like soup, and that's only the beginning of the controversy.

At one time I suppose there was a single recipe, and goulash was as definable and as recognizable as chicken cacciatore or macaroni and cheese. In his notes on *gulays*, international restauranteur George Lang says, "A strange thing has happened to Hungarian gulays. The origin of the soup can be traced back to the ninth century, when shepherds cut their meat into cubes, cooked it with onion in a heavy iron kettle and slowly stewed until all the liquid evaporated. They dried the remnants in the sun and then put the dried food in a big bag made of sheep's stomach. Whenever they wanted to eat, they took out a piece of the dried meat, added some water and reheated it." (From *The Great Cooks Cookbook*.)

I'll bet that, right away, those shepherds started messing with the recipe, adding more water, some broth and a few herbs, or substituting beef for mutton. Over the last 1,000 years or so, cooks have added their own ingredients or taken out things they didn't like until the word "goulash" has become synonymous with "unidentifiable."

Compare these two recipes, both called goulash in separate cookbooks:

- onions browned in lard, beef chunks, diced beef heart, garlic, caraway seeds, paprika, one fresh tomato, Italian peppers, hot cherry pepper pods and potatoes, all served with dumplings.
- diced carrots, diced potatoes, peas, red beans, hamburger and tomato sauce.

Another cookbook says the dish can be made with lamb, veal, or beef, but is adamant about the addition of sour cream and paprika to the tomato sauce base.

Can these all be goulash?

My dad prefaced any reference to goulash with the word "slumgullion," a word I thought he made up, but which I recently learned is in the dictionary. It comes from French words meaning "slime" and "cesspool," and means "a meat stew." (I think, like snafu, it's a World War II soldier's invention, possibly a reflection on Army food.) When Dad used to ask, "What's for supper? Slumgullion goulash?" it was all in fun, not a slam on Mom's cooking. I did find a depression era recipe for slumgullion that calls for a pound of bacon (it was poor man's food then) elbow macaroni, onions and canned tomatoes. Maybe that's goulash, too.

I make goulash in a skillet with hamburger, green pepper and onion, canned tomatoes, elbow macaroni and a can of condensed tomato soup, which is the right way. Some people say that is really Johnny Marzetti, but the fact is, Johnny Marzetti, or "Mazetti," as it is also spelled, contains Cheddar cheese and is baked in the oven. Or so the book says.

Now that that's settled, let's talk about whether the toilet paper should hang on the over the front or back of the roll.

2
This tops everything

I've figured out why there's no room for leftovers in my refrigerator. It's full of stuff to put on top of leftovers to make them palatable.

Where did all those topping come from? What was in my mind when I bought salad mustard, sweet and tangy mustard, and horseradish mustard when we already had a perfectly good jar of that brand the guys in the limousine ask for? All the mustard jars are half-full, lined up on the shelves of the refrigerator door like squat little soldiers in brown and yellow uniforms.

Summer is to blame for part of the problem. Besides the mustard, there is a bottle half-full of ketchup and also a picnic squeeze bottle of ketchup. What's a grilled hot dog without ketchup? For that matter, what's a hot dog without relish, pickles (dill, gherkins and bread and butter) and chopped onion? There are four – yes, four—zipper bags in the egg compartment, each containing half an onion and assorted onion scraps.

Then there's my attempt at healthy eating – mayonnaise in regular, light and fat-free – and four kinds of salad dressing, bought in the hope they would make me like eating salad.

It's all necessary, of course. We couldn't get by without soy sauce, Worcestershire or salsa. We use a tablespoon of them – oh, every three or four months. There's a little plastic cup of barbecue sauce and one of honey mustard brought home from a restaurant under the pretense that it would be consumed, but really we were too cheap to throw away something that came with a dinner that expensive. The same is true for the cups of pizza bread stick dipping sauce, stacked two deep, waiting to be turned into English muffin pizzas someday, although no one in the family likes English muffin pizzas.

All these relishes are designed to make food taste better, and thanks to the miracles of modern science and heaps of sodium, they won't spoil for a year. There's seafood cocktail sauce in there, the remaining half of what was purchased with the New Year's shrimp. Maybe it will be used at the Labor Day company picnic.

I bought chili sauce to put on corned beef hash because that's the way it used to be served in the college dining room where my husband and I met and fell in love, but somehow it's not the same anymore – the chili sauce, I mean. The bottle's almost full.

If all those sauces, dressings and condiments aren't enough, there are the real essentials – homemade raspberry and strawberry jam, fudge sauce for ice cream, Parmesan cheese for the pasta, a half-full jar of spaghetti sauce, and two containers of sour cream, both with a spoonful taken out.

With all those toppings and complements, our food should taste wonderful. The problem is, there's no food. Where would I put it? I've got a plan to clean it all out, though. The next time someone asks for a hamburger with everything, they're going to get it.

3
Give us this day our daily soft, inside slices

The empty lunchbox loomed large on the countertop, waiting for something – anything – to go inside.

"How about ham and cheese?" I asked my son. He had only had it twice that week, and it was already Wednesday.

"OK," he said reluctantly, looking hopefully into the cookie jar.

I rummaged in the cupboard for a fresh loaf of bread, but it wasn't there. At the bottom of one wrapper I found one slice of bread and the predictable end pieces.

"We're almost out of bread," I said. "You'll have to eat a crust."

He made a sour face, and I could tell he was seriously debating the merits of a bread crust sandwich over two-day-old pizza.

I dug a little farther into the cupboard. There, in another wrapper, was another slice of bread, also preserved between two crusts. "Saved from a fate worse than death," I said and noted the look of relief on his face.

Bread crusts. They're the ultimate symbol of poverty and deprivation. Eating stale bread crusts is even worse than having nothing, if literature serves us. Bread crusts are the food of Dickens' street waifs and Solzhenitsyn's gulag prisoners. Adventurers go hungry and we envy their stoicism. Crusaders shun completely the comfort of food and become legends for their sacrifice. But the poor and the despised eat crusts and we are embarrassed for them.

It's hard for me to identify with my children in this loathing for the first and last slice of bread from the loaf. When I was a kid, the crusty end of the loaf was the best part in my estimation, but of course, I'm talking about the homemade bread. Because we were poor, we were forced to eat bread my mother baked at home (oh, the shame). "Sack bread," as I called it, the commercial, white, packaged bread from the store, was a rare treat.

I don't know how my children got into the habit of not using the crusts. It must be my fault. It's always the mother who's to blame when kids are finicky, isn't it? When the kids were small I made grilled cheese sandwiches by putting the crusts back to back, cheese in between, and buttered the cut side before toasting them. That worked until the age of reason overtook them – and they also got tired of grilled cheese.

Because of all the preservatives in today's commercial bakery products, bread crusts taste just like the rest of the loaf. They aren't tough or crusty but the psychological factors remain despite logic. You might as well ask my family to eat the wrapper.

There is one good use for bread crusts, however, and that's as filler for meatloaf. Of course, one child doesn't like meatloaf, either. Could it be it's because he can taste the bread crusts inside?

4
Call it like you see it

My husband came to the table sniffing the air.

"What are you cooking? Did the toast burn?"

"No, I've made something special for breakfast. I browned the oatmeal in a dry, hot skillet before I cooked it to improve the texture and add a nutty flavor."

"I don't want any oatmeal."

That's when I pulled out my ace in the hole. "I found the recipe in your Paul Prudhomme cookbook. It's supposed to be wonderful." By deferring to the expert, I figured I could change my husband's perspective on what really was nothing but plain old oatmeal.

He was unconvinced and I don't think he ever tried the new dish, but it didn't stop me from playing mind games when pushing food on my family. Eating is largely psychological in our society. We don't eat because we're hungry, but because it's time to eat, or it smells good, or looks good, or everyone else is doing it. Why shouldn't a mother use that to her advantage?

When the kids were small, I was always looking for inexpensive, nourishing food. Fried cornmeal mush fits the category, but I knew exactly what would happen if I put a plate of it in front of them and said, "This is mush. Eat it. It's good for you." The name just doesn't have much consumer appeal.

Instead, when I put the browned slices on the table for the first time, I waited for the question.

"What is it?"

"Indian corn cakes," I said enthusiastically. "You can eat them plain, or you can put maple syrup on them." The ploy worked and we ate many a fried mush breakfast surrounded by romantic images of Native Americans grinding corn, and boiling maple sap in huge cauldrons. I don't think of it as being manipulative, only creative. In the same way, broccoli stalks became trees to be uprooted by the giant and stuffed whole into his gaping maw. (If you can put up with a few indelicacies at the table, your kids can eat pretty well.)

All such tactics result in only temporary victories. I've had some success getting my family to try new things without prejudice by presenting the food in a particularly positive light, but the truth is, unless they actually like it, they won't continue to eat it, regardless of its coming to the table in a fancy serving dish.

Then there's the problem that I don't like to cook food I don't like to eat, and I haven't yet found a good way to trick myself.

5
The Tao of brownies

Life is like a batch of brownies.

There are many recipes, each one requiring a certain skill level, but there is no substitute for the right ingredients. Sure, you can get by with just about anything you've got, and someone (usually those who don't appreciate quality or who hope to gain something through flattery) is sure to rave about how good it is, but for the genuine article, you have to have the right stuff. The good news is, it's all readily available.

It takes a little work to come out with a good product. You have to plan ahead, decide what you want and take enough time to combine everything in proportion. It involves work, sometimes sacrifice, and the gratification is way out in the future compared.

Some hard lumps come along, and they have to be beaten out by one process or another. Then, just about the time everything is all smooth and sweet and leveled out, it all goes into the oven and the heat is on. The heat is certainly trying, but without enough of it, and if it isn't hot enough, you get something that's half-baked and won't stand up to the stress of deep cuts. It's the heat that firms, shapes, and produces the reactions among the basic elements that result in the desired product.

Then comes a cooling-down period, a time of rest when things settle, change, and take on a more permanent shape. A few cracks and wrinkles develop on the surface, but underneath, there's richness.

When the cuts are made, it can be a shock – deep slashes that divide the whole just when it seemed all was complete, but the cuts are absolutely necessary for the enjoyment and satisfaction of all. That was the plan all along.

Perfection is rare. Sometimes edges get a little crusty, corners get dry, portions aren't equal, middles are mushy. Why? Carelessness along the way, too little sweetness, too much stirring, cheap substitutions, a moment of inattention when the heat was most severe. Still, it has to be pretty bad before it should be labeled a disaster and discarded.

All too soon, it seems, the pan is empty, and there are nothing but crumbs on the plate. Sometimes there is a bitter aftertaste, a feeling of dissatisfaction and a lack of fulfillment. But when it's good, the memory is as wonderful as the anticipation. The aroma lingers, the flavor hangs on, the enjoyment goes beyond the act.

Life is short; eat dessert first.

How To Eat Like a Child

1
Power of suggestion

He walks to the kitchen, opens the refrigerator and looks at the contents – again!

How long since the last time? Five minutes? Three? He's been there at least five times in the last hour. Since his last inspection, no one has bought groceries or cooked anything. He apparently hopes that through spontaneous generation – some kind of culinary big bang – something new, or at least something more interesting, has appeared on the shelves.

Nothing. The door closes with a soft "whoosh," like the sound of wind across an empty prairie or the sigh of a rejected lover.

Next he moves to the cupboard near the toaster, opens it and inspects the bread. There are still no cookies, except plain old brown windmills. No bags of chips or corn curls.

Methodically he closes the two doors, using both hands. He opens the cereal cabinet, again using both hands, hanging on them with just enough force to keep them open at the center.

Nope. Nothing in there either. He moves on to the canned goods, then the baking supplies, inspecting without comment or emotional commitment, like a well-trained auditor.

The route is completed, but the longing is unsatisfied. He returns to the television, stares without seeing for a moment, channel surfs, sighs, and before long, his gaze strays once more to the kitchen. I sense his restlessness as a thought takes shape in his brain: something was overlooked on his last mission, but what? Like a trial lawyer or a medical research scientist, he waits for inspiration to strike, for the missing clue to manifest itself, but the facts are a dry wasteland. There's nothing in the house he wants to eat. Within minutes, however a call as undeniable as the homing instinct of migratory birds begins to gnaw at him.

He's at the refrigerator – again!

"What are you looking for?" I ask through clenched teeth.

He shrugs. "I don't know. Something."

"Are you hungry?"

Another shrug as he closes the door and moves on to the cabinets. "Dunno. Maybe."

"What do you want? Never mind, I can guess. You don't know. How about a pizza?"

His face brightens. "Yeah! A pizza. That's what I want. Will you fix it?"

It always works, and the thought that I've been manipulated crosses my mind. One of these days I'm going to make a real effort not to offer anything and just see how many trips he'll make through the kitchen before giving up.

Or that could be a bad idea. That refrigerator door is no longer under warranty.

2
When you're older, you'll understand

They tell me childhood obesity is on the increase. I can't figure out why. Children have no neutral gear in their transmissions. They spend years at a stretch in drive. What's more, kids have to beg for every scrap of food they get.

For example, what happens when some poor child comes in from a soccer game or two hours in the swimming pool, about to expire?

"Mom, can I have a cookie?" he asks.

"What do you say?"

"Please, please, *please* can I have a cookie?"

"*May* I have a cookie?"

"May I have a cookie, *pleeease*. I'm starving."

"It's pretty close to lunch time," Mom observes. "Maybe we should wait."

"Can't I have a cookie? Just one? I'll eat lunch, I promise!"

"Well, have you had any other snacks this morning?"

At this point, the child is thinking her next question might be, "And where were you on the night of August 18, 1999, and can anyone confirm your story?"

"Never mind, I'll wait 'til lunch," the child says, tightening his belt another notch.

Mom smiles smugly. "I didn't think you were really very hungry." She helps herself to another cup of coffee and two cookies and sits down with the latest edition of "Reader's Digest" as her offspring goes outside and gets on his bike.

Kids are no easier on each other. If one comes out with Popsicles, he most often will hide them behind his back.

"Which hand?" he asks the drooling sibling or friend. The other one takes a guess and the holder quickly switches the pops. "Nope. Guess again." Meanwhile the pops are dripping onto the deck or the sidewalk, and by the time the game is over, there are about two licks left on the stick.

Can a child leave the living room to get his own snack without also getting treats for everyone in the family? Not likely. The phrase, "While you're up, get me..." should be accompanied by a small wheelbarrow. Even regular mealtimes are preceded by washing up, setting the table and lengthy prayers, and what does the kid get for his trouble? Nasty things like sweet potatoes and lima beans.

If you think adulthood is marked by the right to vote, bear arms and drink alcohol, think again. The truly mature individual has free access to the refrigerator.

3
Gourmet – not

I came across a bargain at the grocery store the other day so I bought something I don't usually buy – refrigerated biscuit dough.

After so many years married to a man raised in the mountains of Virginia, I have come to be a pretty good biscuit baker, if I say so myself. I use fresh buttermilk and Martha White self-rising flour and everyone likes them. The grocery store variety is second-best, for occasional use only – or so I thought.

When I came in with the groceries, my youngest dived into the bags as usual. Coming up with the cans of dough, he yelled, "Oh, boy! Canned biscuits!" He ran to tell the others. You would have thought he had discovered gold.

For some reason, my children seem addicted to cheap food. When I make homemade macaroni and cheese, full of good Cheddar and American cheese, baked until bubbly in the oven, they usually say, "It's all right, Mom, but I like the box kind better."

I consider myself a good cook, but after spending all afternoon making spaghetti sauce from tomatoes right out of the garden, fresh basil and hand-pressed garlic, it's no fun to hear, "What happened? Did you run out of the kind in the jars?" Yes sir, kids recognize quality, and they will reject it every time.

Homemade cakes are not as good as Little Debbies, homemade cookies are not as good as Oreos, homemade potato salad is not as good as the deli variety, homemade soups are not as good as what comes in cans. Kids are connoisseurs in reverse.

If there were food critics for kids, I can only imagine what they would say. "Hmmmm," says one, biting into a spoonful of boxed skillet-dinner lasagna. "Flat, and just a bit chewy, with a certain doughiness that eludes the senses. I love the way the excess salt balances the acidic edge added by the preservatives. Yes, I would say this is about a 1998, an excellent year for powdered sauce mix, probably purchased on sale, perhaps from the damaged goods cart, from the southeast, but not beyond the city limits."

Another, chewing modestly: "I detect just the right amount of added sugar, corn syrup and MSG. None of those herbs that tend to lighten the flavor, just a familiar, satisfying lump in the pit of the stomach."

I did get a good response with homemade bread the other day. It was honey whole wheat, perfectly textured and browned just to toastiness. The kids ate some as soon as it came out of the oven and agreed it was great.

Then somebody said, "You know, mom, you could save yourself a lot of work if you just bought the frozen dough instead."

4
Child's guide to eating spaghetti

First, put on a clean shirt. Never come to the table on spaghetti night wearing the T-shirt that is already covered with finger paint, worm guts, dog hair, ice cream drips and peanut butter finger-stripes. For spaghetti, you need something fresh, preferably white and hard to wash.

Next, ask for a lot. Hold your plate up high and look like those kids in the magazine ads who are begging for food, but be happy. Moms like that, and they will heap the plate full. Sometimes, when you are taking your plate back, the whole serving will slide off onto your lap or the table. Probably it will only happen once, because parents have long memories about stuff like that and they won't let you hold your own plate again until you're 23, so if it happens to you, savor the moment.

Once you actually have the spaghetti, it's time to experiment. Remember, regardless of what the experts say, there isn't any foolproof way to eat spaghetti. If you do the Long Noodle Slurp, you clean off all the sauce. If you roll the spaghetti on your fork, all the chunky stuff gets left behind. If you try to scoop it up, the ends dangle and paint your face, which if fun, but you may get sent away from the table.

If at all possible, invite somebody your own age for dinner, because it's always more fun to eat spaghetti with a friend. You can have noodle races to see who can inhale a single strand the fastest, argue over who gets the crusty piece of garlic bread, and sneak sideways glances at each other and giggle while the noodles are hanging out of the corners of your mouth.

The truly amazing thing about eating spaghetti is that parents don't seem to notice you. They are too busy trying to appear dignified, carefully winding the noodles, trying to carry on a conversation without breathing garlic in anybody's face, and wiping their mouths with napkins between sentences. Every now and then they jump up and run to the kitchen to put cold water and stain remover on the red spots on their clothes. Grownups are boring.

After you actually start feeling hungry, chop the spaghetti up and eat it with a spoon. You'll be done in 30 seconds, just in time for dessert.

5
Try this (only) at home

I looked up from my coffee just in time to see my son lower a cereal bowl from his mouth.

With milk dripping from his chin, he said, "Don't worry, Mom. I only do this at home."

Once we were having pancakes for breakfast and I went to get my son a fork.

"I don't need one," he said.

"You don't need a fork to eat pancakes? Why not?"

"'Cause I just roll them up and eat them out of my hand," he said, and proceeded to turn them into buttered cigars.

I suppose I've fostered a double standard in my children, the concept that some things are all right at home, but nowhere else.

"At home, we love you even if you're a slob," I've said, with good intentions. "Be on your best behavior when you're away because other people might not be willing to overlook your bad manners, and they might never get to appreciate your good qualities."

Table manners are a cultural thing, and it's hard to know just how much to demand. If you drop a cookie on a clean floor and no one's around to see you, is it all right to pick it up and eat it? Scientific studies have been done on this topic. Should one set the table with silver and china to eat alone, just to preserve civilization? Read *Lord of the Flies* and see if you change your mind either way.

In some countries, it's polite to belch and slurp while eating so the cook knows you appreciate the food. Perfectly civilized people who wouldn't think of sitting down at their dining room table without wearing a tie, let alone without utensils, can walk around a park wearing a tank top and munching on a chicken leg at the shop picnic or the soccer game. Table manner standards are at least double, and probably more.

The best host is one who makes guests feel at ease, regardless of custom. Maybe the important thing for kids to learn is the best manners are those that don't offend.

Robert Frost wrote, "Home's the place where, when you have to go there, they have to take you in." It's nice to know there's some place in the world where you can drink out of the milk carton, crumble crackers in your soup and lick jam from your fingers and know your actions won't be seen as the definition of your entire character.

6
'Single serving' defined by the eater

In the book *Personality Plus*, author Florence Littauer relates an incident that began to show her how great were the differences between her and her mate. On their honeymoon, she writes, she was lounging in the sun, eating grapes from a large bunch, when her new husband became distressed. He informed her that if she continued picking randomly at the grapes, the appearance of the bunch would be spoiled. He pulled out his multi-implement key chain and showed her the "right way," snipping off a small stem with the nail clippers so she could it, then snipping off another small stem, progressing in an orderly fashion through the whole bunch..

"I didn't know there were grape rules," she said.

I thought about that little story when I saw my son sit down with nearly two pounds of grapes and a book.

"Remember the grape rules," I said teasingly, "or you'll wind up with an ugly bunch with holes all over it."

He looked confused. "But I'm going to eat them all," he said.

That was one point that escaped Mr. Littauer. The grape rules – or the cookie rules or the chocolate milk rules or the pizza rules – are irrelevant when dealing with young appetites.

Mr. Littauer also would not have needed to invent cottage cheese rules – something like "half a cup served on lettuce with sliced peaches" – if he had lived at my house.

I had just purchased a new 16-ounce carton of cottage cheese when my son said he wanted a snack. "Have some cottage cheese," I said.

He headed for the kitchen and returned a few minutes later, the container in one hand and a spoon in the other, and said, "Can I finish this?"

"Don't be silly," I said. "That's a full carton."

He peered into the depths at approximately an inch of cottage cheese remaining on the bottom. "Not any more," he said.

My husband makes a holiday treat called black bottom pie. The primary ingredients are semi-sweet chocolate, whipping cream and eggs. It's made in a 10-inch spring-form pan the size of a large cheese cake with a graham-cracker and brown sugar crust. We usually figure anywhere from 14 to 16 servings from a pie.

One year the special dessert, still uncut, was cooling in the kitchen when we were getting ready to go out for the evening. In answer to a last minute question from one of the boys, we said yes, he could have a piece while we were gone.

When we came home, we saw a large empty space where pie should have been. We wondered if company had come while we were out.

"You said I could have a piece," said my son. "That's all I had." True. He had cut the pie into four pieces and eaten one of them.

The words "help yourself" should never be uttered in jest, and never if you want to keep some for another day. The term "single serving" means something entirely different to kids than to parents.

To Market, to Market

1
Adult education

It was National Take Your Husband to the Grocery Store Day, so I dragged mine out the door and toward the car.

"I'd really rather work on the lawnmower," he grumbled.

"This is good for you," I said. "It will build your self-esteem. For too long you've thought of the grocery store as just some place where your paycheck goes. It's time you learned the place offers potential for your own self-expression."

Not that my husband has never been to the grocery store, but he thinks of it as a self-serve warehouse for tortilla chips and salsa, sardines, Oreos, teriyaki sauce and charcoal. He has never considered it in an occupational sense.

After we settled the argument about who would push the cart, he said, "Didn't you bring a list? I've heard you save a lot of money by shopping with a list."

I sighed. "Lists limit you, dear. Give up your preconceived grocery prejudices. By starting with the advertised specials, you develop culinary creativity."

"Is that what you do? See what's on special and build your menus around it?"

"Of course."

"That's why we had oxtail and sauerkraut soufflé last week, right?"

"Never mind that. Get a flyer and let's get shopping." I had barely finished teaching him not to select ice cream until he was ready to enter the checkout line when I realized he had started cutting out the little "buy one get one free" squares with the tiny scissors that pop up out of his 27-unit pocket knife.

"Don't depend on technology," I warned. "You never know when a coupon may present itself. In the grocery world, you have to develop survival skills. Here, I'll show you the professional method." I laid the sheet of paper along the sharp edge of a cereal box and neatly ripped apart the rows of coupons.

After we'd loaded the trunk with groceries, I said, "There! Wasn't that exciting? Don't you think you'd like to be a shopper yourself someday?"

"Personally, I like buying better than shopping," he said. "Which is the bag with the sardines? I want some before I start working on the lawn mower."

2
Lose-lose situation

I went to the grocery store and got a birthday card, some flashlight batteries and a frozen pizza. It took two hours and 37 minutes.

No, I didn't have a problem making my selections. That took about 14 minutes, though I will say prices on the frozen pizza were a bit confusing because the two brands on special didn't weigh the same. No, the time was lost in the checkout lane.

There were about a dozen cash register lanes, three of which were manned by clerks. Two of the lines were very long, but at the third lane, the clerk was filing her nails and yawning. Naturally I headed in her direction.

I was momentarily distracted by a headline in the magazine rack informing me that Oprah really is going to get married after all, as soon as she loses a few pounds, and a woman with two carts and three children stepped in ahead of me. What could I say? I know what it's like to shop with kids.

After a short wait as the management called in heavy equipment to handle her purchases, I noticed that one of the other lines was down to only two shoppers, one of whom had only a few items. I got in line behind them just as the lady at the head of the line was pulling out her checkbook. Along with it came the coupons.

The cashier leafed through the customer's stack of coupons, discounting item after item. They discussed expiration dates and whether the item qualified for discount since it was already on sale. There hasn't been a negotiation session like that since we bought Alaska from the Russians.

I noticed the people who had been at the end of the long lines when I first came were now pulling out of the parking lot, and I decided to change lanes again. The woman ahead of me was just handing her check to the cashier. The check didn't clear. As the clerk tried the transaction again, and the woman counted her cash to see whether she could take home her groceries or not, I saw the marathon shopper with the three kids leaving the store, the coupon shopper tipping the bag boy as he closed the trunk, and the woman who had been in front of me a moment ago waving to the manager as she went out the door.

Believe me when I say the expressway isn't the only place where lane changes are risky.

3
Sticker shock

Remember Lil' Abner? He and his under-clad, curvaceous wife, Daisy May, epitomized poverty in America, but they did seem to eat well.

Daisy was constantly plunking down Thanksgiving-sized platters heaped with pork chops in front of her ungainly husband. Where I come from, pork chops cost upwards of $3 a pound and for some cuts, more than $4 a pound. The comic strip cliché for Appalachian poverty has today become a trademark of the rich.

Leaf through a World War II-vintage cookbook. There are all kinds of recipes that save sugar by substituting honey. When I checked the other day, all-purpose varieties of honey cost from $1.75 to $2 a pound, compared with about 40 cents a pound for sugar. The clear golden, honey was close to $3 a pound. Food values have flip-flopped.

This could make the experience of dining out a lot different.

"Oh, look at the variety on this menu," a wife might say to her hubby. "Look! Can you believe this? Peanut butter, by the spoonful or on crackers. Do you know how much peanut butter costs? I paid $2.29 for a jar of it just the other day. I wonder if I should indulge."

"Why not try the cheese?" hubby might counter. "Can you believe that when my grandmother served it with macaroni every Friday night I used to turn up my nose? Yes, I think the cheese would be nice. After all, we don't eat out every day."

The wife snuggles close and says. "Sardines. Such luxury." She follows the price column to a real whopper and croaks. "Spam! It's at least four dollars a pound in the store. I see they're offering a two-ounce serving. No, it's too much. Even if it is our anniversary, we have to be practical. I'll just have the steak."

Meanwhile, across town in a poorer neighborhood, an unemployed mother of three is dishing up 99-cent-per-pound chicken to her children who groan and say, "What, chicken again? Can't we ever have tuna?"

"I'm sorry, dears," she sighs, "It's just too expensive."

4
Thanks for shopping with us. See you in an hour.

I heard that woman on the radio again, the one who cooks enough meals in one day to feed the family for a whole month. I was so inspired I made a double batch of lasagna, thinking I would freeze the extra for another day. Someone ate the second batch during a TV commercial break.

Forget cooking ahead. I can't even *buy* ahead. I'm always amazed at the accounts of pioneers who took the wagon into town twice a year for supplies. If I did that, I would need a refrigerator as big as Yankee Stadium, and it would have to be guarded by armed Pinkerton employees or the food would be gone in a week.

The food just vanishes. Frozen pizzas ooze through the walls of the freezer when I'm not looking. Potato chips disappear as people walk past the pantry, as if carried along on the breeze. Sandwich meats melt into breakfast omelets and are absent-mindedly consumed by those staring into the refrigerator wondering what to eat. Though it hasn't been proven in laboratories, milk apparently evaporates at the rate of one gallon per half-hour in homes where one or more teenagers reside.

Appetite expands to equal the amount of food available. The more I cook, the more we eat. The faster I cook, the faster we eat. If I want cookies for lunches on Monday, I have to bake them Sunday night after everyone else is in bed. Not only are the cookies eaten as desert and snacks, the dough is eaten before it ever hits the oven.

Just about the time I get some meals made ahead, or even some extra groceries on the shelf, unexpected company comes. On a Saturday not long ago, our family and four of the kids' friends (that's a total of 8 guys and me) consumed a dozen buttermilk biscuits, 20 pieces of grilled chicken, a bowl of scalloped potatoes, a whole cake, 15 large ground beef barbecue sandwiches, one and a half bags of chips, two and a half quarts of juice, a gallon and a half of milk, two boxes of cereal, a dozen cookies and assorted snacks.

Everyone had such a good time that they stayed overnight. On Sunday we ate half a ham, another dozen biscuits, three pounds each of potatoes and carrots, three pizzas, a loaf of bread and assorted goodies. That was all after breakfast. The friends all went home before supper. I think they noticed the walls of the refrigerator beginning to collapse due to the vacuum that had been created inside.

My mother lived alone while my children were growing up. She had two freezers that were always jam-packed with food, and hundreds of quarts of canned vegetables on the shelves of her small home. That gives me hope. As soon as there's no one around to eat, I'll be able to cook ahead, too.

5
The last (minute) supper

We shoppers milled about with glazed eyes, passing the canned beef stew and boxed potato entrees, headed we knew not where, haunted by the sure knowledge that suppertime was coming.

We had a vague notion that somewhere between the prepackaged Oriental stir-fry mix and the ready-to-eat breaded chicken patties there was an idea for supper, but we had not found it yet. We kept moving, compelled by a force greater than our collective self, lemmings on the way to a culinary cliff.

You've seen those movies where an asteroid is on a collision course with earth and can't be stopped, or the volcano is about to erupt, or a nuclear holocaust is about to be unleashed. Disaster is imminent. People are trying to use their last minutes to create something worthwhile, but time is running out. There's a lot of crying and soul-searching and general confusion, and people trudge along aimlessly, still hoping deliverance will appear. The action in the grocery store at 5:30 p.m. is a lot like that.

Stopping on the way home from work to pick up something for supper has become a way of life, except for those few who commute by helicopter. There are a lot of reasons, I suppose – the artificial meal schedules imposed by an industrial society, the marketing gurus who tell us if we serve something as simple as tomato soup and bread and butter for supper, our children will someday turn to blowing up federal buildings to express their rage at deprivation. The hectic pace of two- and three- and four-job families makes eating a chore and grocery shopping a nightmare. The reasons don't matter. Suppertime comes, just like death and taxes, whether you are prepared or not.

For years I was ashamed to admit I was in the grocery store between 5 and 5:30 p.m. trying to find something I could put on the table that looked homemade within 15 minutes of my arrival at home. Good mothers, I thought, have menu lists magnetized to the refrigerator door and supplies to make the meals. They make supper the night before, and walk in the door from work to the aroma of lemon and herb chicken simmering in the slow cooker, or meat loaf in the timer-started oven. The afternoon grocery store scenario is where all the bad mothers of the world congregate to try to make up for their ineffectiveness.

"I'm not really shopping for supper," I would tell the clerk as I went through the checkout with a bag of ready-mixed salad, frozen garlic bread, and four cans of Franco-American spaghetti with meatballs. "This is for a food collection for the poor I just heard about."

I no longer lie. I just wear a Halloween mask and hope I don't bump into anyone I know. When I can't avoid a friend, I listen to her excuses and she listens to mine, and we both politely pretend this hurried trip is out of the ordinary.

A lot of women in the store obviously just came from work, unless they just like to put on high heels and makeup to come in and browse the damaged canned goods rack. There are a lot of men in work attire who are shopping, too, but they get to use the excuse that their wife called and asked them to stop on the way home.

A lot of literature is given over to the plight of the unprepared – the grasshopper and the ant, for instance, or the New Testament parable of the virgins who had no oil for their lamps. Last-minute supper buyers have to live with their faults, and when disaster strikes, we will be highly recognizable. We'll be the ones rushing home from 7-11 with a quart of milk so our families can have cold cereal for our last supper.

Ahhhh, la carte!

1
Puffed with pride

 I had just finished making what was probably my four- millionth batch of marshmallow and rice cereal snacks when I was struck by the amazing diversity of the marshmallow. I mean, how many things can you name that taste good with both yams and chocolate? It seems natural to us now, but think about other possible combinations – jelly beans on toast, or potato chips dunked in coffee. The marshmallow-cereal combination should be nominated for a Nobel Prize.

 The origins of marshmallow candy have apparently been lost. It's associated with the marsh mallow, a coastal swamp plant imported from Britain, the roots of which were once used to make "sweetmeats," as the British say. It's unclear, however, whether marshmallows got their name for the flavor or because the little puffs resemble the shape of the sliced roots.

 Wherever they came from, marshmallows are a wonderful invention, right up there with hair spray and the retractable ballpoint pen. You can do anything with marshmallows. One of the greatest party games I ever saw was a contest to see who could get the most marshmallows in their mouth without swallowing any. Not long ago at my son's birthday party, sophisticated adults got pretty wild creating jewelry from duct tape and colored marshmallows – including a jewel in the navel. At Easter time, some people do marshmallow drops from planes instead of hiding eggs. In a pinch, you can use marshmallows to stick pictures on the wall.

I think the possibilities are limitless. How about throwing miniature marshmallows at weddings instead of rice or birdseed? All the children in the crowd would eat them, and there would be nothing for the church custodian to clean up. How about a car that runs on marshmallows? The only exhaust would be those little white puffs, and they would dissolve in the first good rain.

I suspect that melted marshmallows would sop up oil spills. Pour the marshmallow cream on the troubled waters and it would mix with the oil, just as it does with margarine in the saucepan. If a few plane loads of rice cereal were thrown on top and the whole thing rolled into a log, it could be sliced and sold at the concession stand at school sporting events. (Those clinical studies showing that petroleum consumption by humans is dangerous are probably unreliable, and besides, very little of the stuff bought from concession stands is eaten. Everything ends up under the bleachers and can easily be swept up.)

The next time someone calls you a marshmallow, thank them, and while you're at it, ask them to pass the cereal.

2
Just plain food

There's a good reason why we don't have more homemade goodies around our house. The fact is, they are eaten by degrees before they ever come to completion.

Occasionally the baking bug bites on a Saturday morning or an evening after a leisurely dinner, and I decide to make a family favorite like apple cobbler. When the apples are peeled and sliced, spiced and sugared and ready in the pan, and the butter is cut into the flour and sugar for the topping, I go to the refrigerator and get the last egg and take out the gallon milk container.

There are one and a half teaspoons of milk in it.

Having milk available for such spontaneous occasions in a house where there are two teenagers and a 10-year-old is quite a trick. If I want to bake on Saturday, I have to buy milk on Saturday. Buying it on Friday is useless, especially if we also have cold cereal on hand.

Well, chocolate chip cookies require no milk, and the ingredients are common: flour, sugar, butter, eggs, a little soda and salt, and then the *piece de resistance*, chocolate chips! I open the drawer where I store things like brown sugar and coconut and walnuts, and there's the chocolate chip bag.

There are three chips inside.

"Who ate the chocolate chips?"

"I only ate a few," says one.

"The bag was open, so I figured you wouldn't mind. I just put a few on ice cream," says another.

"They were almost gone, so I just finished them," said another.

All right, spontaneity doesn't work. I've learned, however, that planning ahead doesn't work either. When I bought cereal and marshmallows for Rice Krispie Treats, the cereal was eaten as a bedtime snack and the marshmallows got microwaved on graham crackers or put on hot chocolate.

Sprinkles for the Christmas cookies get put on ice cream cones. Powdered sugar for icing goes into the hot chocolate mix. Blueberries for the muffins get used in the pancakes. It all goes to the same place eventually, but it's a little like money in an inflationary economy. The components get eaten by degrees, and you never have the satisfaction of seeing a finished product.

I know why zucchini cake became so popular. Zucchini is the one ingredient nobody snitches when you aren't looking.

3
Don't cry! Food's on the way

My husband was cooking something new.

"Smells good," I said. "What is it?"

"Sautéed onions with jalapenos in cayenne sauce," he said. "Want a taste? It's done."

"How can you tell?"

"It's turned black, and the skillet cracked."

I slowly backed away from the stove. "No, thanks. If I had a taste, why, I know I just wouldn't be able to quit, and there might not be enough for everyone."

What I meant was, onions are a guy thing.

I've learned that on those evenings when there's nothing planned for supper, the best thing to do is start frying onions. It doesn't matter whether they will actually be part of the menu. When the satisfying aroma of onions fills the kitchen, all the men in the family think supper is well under way and that it will soon appear, hot and steamy, on the dining room table. When the meal turns out to be Spaghetti-Os with a side of applesauce, it's a little hard to explain what happened to the onions, but they served their purpose.

I've always thought it was significant that after the Israelites escaped the shackles of Egypt, they whined because they missed the leeks. They forgot the beatings and back-breaking labor, the prejudice and deprivation. Only the memory of the rich flavor and aroma of onions filled their minds. What a tribute to the lowly root!

My husband likes onion soup, onions in omelets and on tacos, and in ratio of about one to one with potatoes in hash browns, with or without cheese. He likes them sliced thick on burgers, chopped and spooned onto hot dogs, and boiled whole in stew. He embarrasses me when we eat breakfast in a restaurant by sending back his American fries with a request for more onions. It's a taste he learned at home. His sister and her husband take their own slice of onion when they go out for a burger because fast-food restaurants don't put enough on.

Where onions are concerned, my husband has adopted the motto of Muppet star Miss Piggy: "Too much is never enough." Maybe it's because his name rhymes with onion that my husband is so fond of them. I'm just glad I didn't marry a guy named Marlick.

4
Homemade ice cream leaves me cold

Making homemade ice cream seemed like a good idea at the time. I could envision doing it every summer. Years from now, when the boys were grown up with children of their own, they would lean back after dinner and say, "Boy, I remember when I was a kid how we used to make homemade ice cream. Best stuff in the world. Come on, kids, let's do that ourselves. You'll love it." Oh, how our fantasies entrap us!

After scouring the rust from the freezer (the fact that it hadn't been used in recent memory should have sounded a warning bell), I made the ice cream mix. I blended the milk, eggs and sugar and cooked them just a bit too long, and put in too much cream, but it tasted all right, in spite of the tiny bits of Teflon that flaked off the mixing spoon. After I poured the liquid into the canister and moved to the deck, it was time for The Men to take over.

The crank didn't seem to fit just right, but Dad fixed it with a bigger hammer and loaded the bucket with ice and salt. By then, he was beginning to sweat. The canister would not turn.

Now dad was muttering. He unloaded all the ice and salt, scraped the bottom of the bucket, rechecked the crank and loaded it up again. The canister would not turn.

At this point, the man who makes his living solving mechanical problems stated, "I've got to get away from this," and went into the house.

The kids and I stared at the bucket and kicked it gently. Then from somewhere deep in the recesses of my mind, I dredged up a memory of pouring water into the bucket of ice, so we tried that. The canister turned freely.

Just then Dad reappeared. "I just figured it out," he said. "You have to pour water on the ice. The ice is freezing onto the sides of the canister and making it – " and then he noticed one of the kids already engaged in the churning.

We all thanked him and got on with the real fun of homemade ice cream – turning the crank. The youngest child, who had been as annoying as a mosquito asking how long until he could turn the crank, finally got the opportunity. He worked faithfully for 34 seconds, then announced it was his brother's turn. The teenager who lifts weights and can curl 40 pounds was exhausted after about three minutes. The teenager who does chin-ups on the basketball backboard gave out after about four.

The deck was littered with towels, rock salt, cold water, overturned chairs, utensils and buckets. The kitchen was littered with spoons, bowls and spatulas, and parts of two different freezers. Tthere was ice water puddled on the floor with bits of dirt and rock salt in it.

What had started out as an exercise in family fun had turned into a grudge match pitting myself, my husband and the freezer against one another.. (The boys had long ago wandered off to read, ride bikes and draw.) After cranking for about three hours, we opened the freezer to reveal a product with the consistency of gazpacho, but we couldn't freeze it anymore because the gear on the crank was stripped. We poured it into a bowl and put it in the refrigerator freezing compartment.

Later we all ate some of the ice cream, and it tasted good. It should, at a cost of about $11 a quart, which included four extra bags of ice not used and two cartons of cream used but not needed. The funny thing is, as we licked our spoons, we began to talk about "next time."

Voila! Tradition is born.

5
Swiss Army knife of the food world

When I'm driving on the expressway, my mind tends to wander. Recently, while on the way to pick up my husband from work, my stream of consciousness was running over a conversation I had earlier in the day about food that kids enjoy.

Suddenly I had a vision of my favorite childhood sandwich – peanut butter and Miracle Whip. (Real mayonnaise is no good for peanut butter. You have to have the sweeter, less firm variety of salad dressing.) There's nothing else like it, especially on squishy white bread. I don't know how I happened on the combination, but I ate many a PBMW sandwich in my carefree youth.

It's not the strangest peanut butter duo I've encountered. Some people make their sandwich with peanut butter and pickles (PBP), or peanut butter and onion (PBO), both of which are a long way from the traditional peanut butter and jelly (PBJ).

PBJ seems right to us, but I think that's just social conditioning. It's like the musical *Oklahoma!* We know it's a great story with great music and choreography, but think how strange the name must have seemed to theater goers when it was new. Imagine reading a broadside for *North Dakota!* or finding *Utah!* in the arts calendar. We know *Oklahoma!* is right, and we know peanut butter just naturally goes with all kinds of jam and jelly, but somewhere, sometime, someone probably looked at someone else making a PBJ sandwich and said, "You're going to eat *what*?"

Peanut butter on bananas or apples is a fine, mellow combination. There's also peanut butter and celery, and some like to throw a handful of raisins on top and call it "ants on a log." But if you can eat peanut butter with those fruits and vegetables, why not put it on corn or cantaloupe? I learned from a friend who is a missionary that the Indonesians and other Eastern people top vegetables with peanut sauce, which is little more than thinned peanut butter. So for supper tonight, why not try a PBBP (peanut butter on baked potato)? Maybe it's good.

As a member of a summer camp staff, I learned to eat what was available. One of my favorite meals was Saturday lunch, when the main course was a selection of sandwich fillings. I put them all together to make a peanut butter-mustard-bologna-honey sandwich. It saved time. I still love the combination of peanut butter and cold, sliced bologna, or peanut butter as the topping on a boiled hot dog.

I don't dip into the peanut butter jar as often as I used to. The experts tell me it's too much fat and that peanut butter sticks in the arteries worse than to the roof of your mouth. Still, I occasionally like to indulge in a dab of peanut butter on hot toast with a cup of tea or hot chocolate. I skip the Miracle Whip, and I never touch bologna, but one of these days, just to revive the spirit of adventure, I'm going to reach for the pickles, onions and mustard and find out what I've been missing.

6
Fiction, or something like it

On a cold night I love to curl up with a cup of hot tea and a good cookbook. The characters are marvelous—desperate Scallions and feisty Ginger Root, sweet Rosemary and handsome, debonair Beau Monde.

If I don't happen to have a cookbook in the house that I haven't read yet, a magazine will do, especially one that has menus like chicken dejon with coucous, glazed julienne carrots and Bermuda onions, and arugula salad with mandarin oranges and walnuts topped with raspberry vinaigrette dressing.

Never mind that what we are having for supper is boiled hot dogs without buns, boxed macaroni and cheese, and commercial applesauce served on paper plates with only forks on the table. The recipes and menus I read bear no more resemblance to reality than the events in bodice-ripper romances.

My neighbor once told me, "My daughter is living proof that children don't need vegetables to survive. Amy didn't eat anything green until she was 11."

I understood her remarks after my own first child shot into the 99th percentile on the growth charts on a diet of processed cheese and graham crackers. (Eventually he incorporated bananas when he had to start carrying a lunch.)

Real, natural, unprocessed and unpackaged food is wonderful stuff. The trouble is, it has to be washed, peeled, chopped, cooked, served in a dish, and eaten off plates with silverware, all of which then have to be washed. All the effort and expense associated with real food can still mean a deep scowl of skepticism and a snide comment when the finished product reaches the table, whereas breaded chicken patties and French fries are consumed with glee.

I suppose every family has its own limits on processed food. Some will only eat hot cereal. Some will eat cold cereal, but nothing presweetened. Some will eat cold and presweetened, but not colored. Some will eat cold, presweetened, colored cereals, but reject marshmallows. Some families are content with frozen vegetables, while others eat only fresh. Others eat nothing they don't grow themselves.

I have my standards, too. Just the other day I read a great recipe for tartar sauce that starts with homemade, low-fat mayonnaise. It should be great on frozen fish sticks.

7
When the menu muse has flown

I remember my sister years ago saying, "I wouldn't mind cooking if someone would just tell me what to fix."

Well, I thought, that's pretty silly. Deciding what to prepare is half the fun of cooking. That was true for me – for about 11 years. After that it got difficult, then boring, then desperate.

"What's for supper?" is a question fraught with all kinds of emotional stress. It means, "I'm hungry and I'm depending on you to feed me." It means, "Really good moms plan ahead and have menu lists stuck to the refrigerator doors for all to see." It means, "I sure hope we get something interesting, colorful, tasty, nutritious, inexpensive and filling by the time I hit the next level on this video game." Talk about pressure!

The pressure is compounded when the question is repeated by various family members at four-minute intervals. One child asks, "What's for supper?" and I say something like, "Oh, something good. You'll like it." Then the next one asks, and I say, "You'll be fed. You've never gone to bed hungry yet." The next one gets, "Leave me alone. How can I cook with you nagging at me?"

When the hubby comes in and asks again, it's just too much. "I haven't the foggiest notion what's for supper, and if anybody else asks, there won't be any supper at all, and maybe there'll never be another meal fixed in this kitchen. I'm thinking of turning it into a museum!" That doesn't answer his question, and it sometimes makes him wonder about the identity of that strange woman in front of the sink.

I did some serious grocery buying a while back. I put about 115 pounds of meat in the freezer, and several bags of canned and dry foods on the shelf. Then I stood in the middle of the kitchen, looked around, and wondered what to make for supper.

You know that famous sculpture by August Rodin, the one with the naked man in deep thought, staring fixedly, his head propped on one fist? I think it was inspired by a scenario something like this: Mr. Rodin came in from the granite pits, threw his smock across a chair and said (as usual) "What's for supper?"

It was the last straw for Mrs. Rodin. They had been married somewhere between four and 29 years, and the thrill of creating new menus had peaked long ago. They had reached a point where the only things enjoyed by every member of the family were celery sticks with peanut butter and raisins, and chicken noodle soup with saltines. She had suddenly had enough.

Mrs. Rodin took offer her apron, hung it by the fireplace, turned to her husband and said, "I don't know what's for supper, Auggy. You decide."

I believe that's how "The Thinker" was inspired. It's Mr. Rodin, who turned to stone while trying to decide what to have for supper.

8
Get it while it's hot

Saturday night for supper we had pot roast with vegetables, hamburgers, hot dogs, vegetable soup and nacho chips.

It seems like an odd menu, but the fact is, four people were eating four different leftovers.

Dad had the pot roast since he missed it the first time around. There was just enough hamburger for two patties, so one child had a hamburger and nacho chips and one had a cheeseburger. I had the leftover vegetable soup, accompanied by the last remaining hot dog, microwaved to perfection. Luckily, the other kid was at work.

Leftovers are funny things. Often the things left over are in the refrigerator because no one liked the food enough to eat it when it was fresh and hot on the dinner table. I found some strawberry yogurt the other day that was nearly over the edge. Knowing that no one especially likes strawberry yogurt, but hating to throw it away, I decided to rescue it creatively. I stirred up a package of vanilla pudding, minus some of the milk, then folded in the strawberry yogurt and some whipped topping. I baked a white cake and served it with the strawberry fluff on top, one piece to my husband, one piece to myself. Nobody else wanted it.

Three days later, the plain white cake had all been eaten with ice cream or fudge topping. A week later I threw out a quart of soured strawberry fluff instead of the half-cup of yogurt I didn't want to waste before.

A while ago a friend was helping in the kitchen.

"Shall I put this out for lunch?" she asked, poking a spoon into some cold casserole.

"Well, it's been in the refrigerator for a while and nobody really likes it."

"Why don't you throw it out?" she asked.

"It was expensive to make. I'll keep it for a while," I said. "Then, when it's rotten. I'll throw it out and won't feel so bad."

I once saw one of those old war-time musical comedies where the recruits were having trouble finding enough time to practice their dance routines. Military duties dept interfering. (War is such an inconvenience.) They figured out that cutting down on KP duties would generate the needed hours, so the mastermind decided the camp could no longer have any dirty garbage cans to wash.

"What will we do with the garbage?" asked another soldier.

"Eat it," he said. At every meal, the musical group spread out to coerce their fellow recruits to eat every morsel of food, thus keeping the garbage cans clean.

I think I like that approach. After all, tonight's dinner becomes tomorrow's uneaten snack ... becomes leftovers ... becomes garbage. It's exactly the same food. My advice is, get it while it's hot.

9
Safe soup? Where's the challenge?

Take warning. Soup season is upon us.

Some soup is safe. It comes out of cans and has a published list of measured ingredients. Even if some of those ingredients sound like petroleum derivatives and noxious diseases, the list is controlled, definable, easy to replicate. You can bet that in any can of chicken noodle soup there will be three cubes of chicken, two ounces of noodles and a lot of broth. It never varies.

Homemade soup, on the other hand, is not safe. Homemade soup begins with an urge to clean out the refrigerator. It grows by leaps and bounds as vegetables mutate when exposed to tomato acids and excessive heat. It swells as it soaks up leftover gravies and sauces, meat scraps and lunch box leavings, heaving and swirling in the kettle as it ripens.

Oh, there are those who will get out the recipe book and turn to "Southern Corn Chowder," but just wait until they get down the list of 27 ingredients and find they don't have any shallots. Then what? Once you substitute an onion for a shallot, it's down the slippery slope to substituting canned corn for fresh, then tossing in a few peas to stretch it, then a bowl of leftover macaroni and cheese and the rest of the holiday marshmallows. Who will know? No one analyzes soup.

One cold Saturday I was desperate for a quick lunch and spied a pan of leftover noodles from Friday's supper. I chopped up some leftover chicken (after first giving it the sniff test), then added water – a lot of water – and brought it all to a boil.

Now fully in the soup spirit, I threw in some leftover corn, onions someone had chopped for hash browns and didn't use and all the celery that wasn't completely brown. It was too thick. Add some milk. Now too thin. I'm getting reckless now, cooking with total abandon. Stir in two envelopes of instant cream of chicken soup mix. Add a package of bullion. Oops! Beef bullion! Doesn't matter. Keep going! Stir it in, no one will notice. Douse it with pepper and parsley, turn up the heat, cover it and pretend not to watch it boil.

It tasted marvelous. We ate the whole mess.

In soup, as in life, safe isn't always better. It's when you take the risks that you find the flavor.

10
Sweet taste of failure

I came home one day to find my husband baking a chocolate cake. That day he was trying a new recipe, one he had been eyeing for some time. It was a "from scratch" cake, a recipe from his new cookbook full of recipes compiled by chefs from Stars Restaurant. While the book has lots of elegant offerings with French names, this one seemed pretty sensible – Grandmother's Chocolate Cake, made with cocoa and buttermilk.

He was mixing the batter when I came home. It was a big cake, three layers, and we were short one pan, but that problem was overcome with patience. But looking back, as you do when any crisis is over, that may have been the beginning of the end.

When two pans of batter had baked, my husband turned out the first cake to cool, then the second. They stuck to the pans, but not badly. He then put the rest of the batter in one of the emptied and cleaned pans and put it back in to bake. That one also stuck when it was turned out, gouging out hunks of cake from the bottom.

Perhaps because we were in a hurry, we didn't allow the layers to cool long enough. We will never know. But no problem, we thought. There was lovely chocolate cream icing to conceal the flaws. We knew we were facing a challenge, but that was all right. Chocolate cake is all good.

The icing used about a half-pound of chocolate and a pint of thick cream, and it was smooth and delicious. Unfortunately the cake layers had stuck to the surfaces on which they were cooling, but by using a large spatula, we managed to get one of them onto the cake plate and put a coating of icing on it.

The second layer was more difficult. It cracked into three main pieces when we tried to move it, but we figured pressure from the top layer, coupled with the gooey icing, would keep it all together. I pushed the pieces back together and he applied icing, calling on his years of experience mudding drywall.

The third layer broke, too, but the top layer of icing made it look quite presentable, except that there was a definite Leaning Tower of Pisa effect when the cake was viewed from the side. My husband was using a rubber spatula to finish the icing, blending it with the crumbs. Pieces of cake kept breaking off and falling onto the table and the floor. He finally called it quits, and I volunteered to try my hand at it using a table knife.

It began to look fairly presentable, and I raised one side of the cake plate to see if the off-center layers would slide a bit. They did, in pieces, right off the other layers and onto the table, like chocolate glaciers falling into the sea. Some help I turned out to be!

I mention this incident for two reasons: first, while my husband was down on his knees picking up hunks of cake from the floor, he said, "I don't think I'd mention this if I were you"; and second, it serves as a warning to anyone viewing a failed enterprise.

The casual observer would not know about the delicate chocolate cakes with chocolate gnache he often makes, the perfect pork loin roast in white wine sauce he made the day before, or the cheese and sausage bread he had made on Saturday, gone in 60 seconds. He or she wouldn't know about his locally famous grilled chicken or apple ambrosia pie. There's a big difference between failing and being a failure.

Here is a bit of wisdom: you cannot pick up iced chocolate layer cake and put it back any more than you can put the toothpaste back into the tube. At the end, we got the large metal spatula and scraped the whole cake into a really big bowl. We stuck a mixing spoon in it and scooped the servings out into cereal bowls. Call it failure if you like, but I think we invented something good.

11
If you can't take the heat

It's too hot to cook.

I haven't turned the oven on for so long the gas company thinks I've moved. The microwave hasn't been used for anything in weeks except to boil nectar for the hummingbird feeder. Just the idea of making grilled cheese sandwiches on the electric griddle makes me sweat.

Even if it wasn't too hot to turn on an appliance, it's too hot to eat the food. We've been living on cold stuff, and it's boring. Away with pasta salad! I'm ready for spaghetti and meatballs and lasagna baked in a big pan in the oven. No more potato salad from the deli. I want baked potatoes, so hot you have to put mitts on to handle them.

What I crave is meatloaf with lots of steamy gravy, not cooked in the slow cooker out in the garage, but in a good hot oven. And I don't want to eat it from a paper plate with a plastic fork. I want real dishes that have to be washed in hot water. Picnic-style entertaining has been done to death, and we haven't even had family reunion yet. Burgers on the grill I now consider subsistence fare. I've had my fill of salty hot dogs cooked on a stick, fast-food chicken and Chinese take-out picked up on the way home from work because nobody wants to work in the kitchen. I want tuna casserole and macaroni and cheese and scalloped potatoes – comfort food with aromas wafting through the room while it cools enough to eat.

I'm only half-way through summer, and already it's getting to be too much of a good thing. I waited so long for summer to get here. About mid-March, I was so anxious to get outside and do all the jobs that had accumulated over the cold months. I was aching for the sunshine after a season of gray skies. I got my wish, in a big way. Summer was wonderful, for about two weeks. Now I want relief, and there's none in sight for at least a couple months.

How could this happen? As soon as the first hard, dry tasteless watermelons came on the market after Christmas, we bought a chunk and ate it, pretending it was real, and drooled as we talked about how good the summer melons would be. Now the thought of ice-cold watermelon just makes my teeth ache. Summer? Been there, done that, got the T-shirt covered with barbecue sauce from one too many cookouts.

I'll get through. I'll crank up the air conditioning while I hide from the heat that I longed for only a few months ago, and pretty soon it will be fall. I'm beginning to understand why optimists aren't always appreciated. This endless sunshine is about to drive me crazy.

12
Too much on your plate? Share!

"How's the fish?" I reached across the restaurant table and speared a bit of my husband's entrée.

"Pretty good," he said. After swallowing my sample, I agreed. He said, "How's the steak."

"Not bad," I said. "Want a bite?"

He shook his head, as I figured he would. He doesn't share what's on my plate as much as I share what's on his.

I don't know that I've even seen this particular habit explored in the advice columns or etiquette books. It's probably bad manners, something that should only be done in the privacy of one's own home. I eat off his plate at home, too, usually the leftover hash browns or occasional half-slice of toast, but it's in restaurants where it's most fun. We seldom order the same thing, and I get to sample something new without having to buy a whole dinner.

I suppose it's a mark of trust (maybe that's just another word for familiarity) that I feel free to eat my husband's food, even without asking permission. My relaxed attitude comes partly from knowing that if I said, "Your dinner looks better than mine. Can I have it?" he would immediately say "yes" and trade, if he thought I was serious. Plate sharing without the benefit of an extra plate is close and personal, an act of genuine friendship.

My son began to get protective of his French fries in high school when we took him out for fast food. I never ordered any fries. I just ate some of his.

"You never finish your fries," I said when he complained. "You always order the super size, and then leave a bunch in the wrapper. Why should you care if I eat a few?"

"I just want my own fries," he said. "Why don't you order some for yourself instead of eating mine?"

It was hard to explain. I wanted to bring intimacy and sharing to the picture, elements he was not after at that particular time. He wanted to be farther from Mom, not closer. Having his own fries was a symbol of freedom and independence.

I've often heard men complain that their wives don't order dessert at the restaurant. "I'll just have a bite of yours," they say, and then, most often, they eat the pointy end of the piece of pie, or the extra sauce that runs off the hot fudge brownie. Men who would lay down their lives in defense of their wives against an attacker or force of nature aren't so willing to sacrifice their dessert.

In the book of the Bible that bears his name, we read about Nehemiah, who directed the rebuilding of the wall of Jerusalem and the return of the Jewish people from captivity. His job in Babylon was to be the king's cupbearer. That means he got to taste the king's wine and food before king did. That way, if it was poisoned, Nehemiah died and the king didn't. Nehemiah was expendable. Where do you get the courage for a job like that, or the experience? Maybe he was married and they ate out a lot.

Pot-blessed

1
Covered dish lunch uncovered

No matter what season it is, it's potluck season. Holidays, graduation open house, wedding receptions and picnics are just the excuses Americans need to begin cooking double recipes of everything in case someone else forgets to bring their share.

Of course, no one else ever forgets. Since we are all persuaded that the success of any given potluck rests entirely on our own (picnic ham) shoulders, the amount of food that arrives could usually feed a third world country for at least a day.

The principle of potlucks is that the sum of the parts is greater than the whole. That's impossible in math, but not in the kitchen. Anyone who has made vegetable soup knows that even though you took from the refrigerator only a few wilted carrots, brown celery, the shriveled potatoes, and a week's worth of dried-out meat scraps and vegetable leftovers, you will still come up with a batch of soup so big some of it will have to go into the freezer or back into the refrigerator, leftovers once again reborn. I think I'm beginning to understand the origins of the belief in reincarnation.

Potluck dinners work the same way. I've actually been to some when I went home with more food than I brought, even though I ate my full share.

I'm not sure why potlucks are so popular. Who wants to sit on a folding chair holding a leaky paper plate full of lukewarm alien casserole when he or she could be sitting in the comfort of their own home, at a table, enjoying familiar, hot food? Who knows? It's the party atmosphere, I suppose, and the fun of being together. Men know they will get all kinds of fatty meats and desserts at a potluck that their wives won't allow them to eat at home. Kids can sit down with a plate of macaroni and cheese, scalloped potatoes and Spanish rice and not be chided about eating vegetables. Chances are they won't eat anything except Jell-O and Texas sheet cake, but that's all right at a potluck.

The amount of food consumed at a potluck can be prodigious. At one holiday potluck at the hospital maintenance department where my husband worked, the men brought two 9-inch by 13-inch pans of cornbread (the kind with cheese and peppers and corn mixed in), 26 buttermilk biscuits, 34 deviled eggs, eight pounds of pinto beans cooked with eight pounds of ham, five pounds of mixed beans and beef, 30 meatballs in brown gravy, three cups of salsa, relishes, butter, jam, honey, and a batch of Rice Krispie treats. There were 28 men at the dinner. They ate every scrap of food. It took them one hour. I suspect they all went home and asked their wives for a snack before supper.

Potlucks are the ultimate in sharing. They remind us that no one is so poor they have nothing to give. I once heard singer and author Gloria Gaither speak at a women's conference. She told the story of a single man on a Sunday morning who heard the announcement about the church picnic, to be held that afternoon. "Everyone bring something," the folks were told. The man went home and looked into his bare refrigerator. Nothing there but a couple packets of mustard, some sour milk, and a single slice of bologna, brown and curled at the edges. He found two bread crusts, brushed off a couple spots of mold and made a sandwich, and headed for the picnic.

When he arrived at the park, the meal had already begun. He found an empty folding chair and took the sandwich from its crumpled brown bag and started to take a bite, but then he caught sight of a group of people at a nearby picnic table.

On their table was a platter heaped with fried chicken and sliced ham; a huge bowl of rich, creamy homemade potato salad; trays of deviled eggs; baskets of crusty, brown rolls with apple butter and strawberry jam; plates of bright green pickles and a dish of marinated beans. There was a three-layer chocolate cake in the middle of the table, a pan of banana pudding and an assortment of cookies. There was cold milk and lemonade, and hot coffee in a thermos.

Someone at the table waved. "Hey! Come over," he called. "Put your lunch in with ours. We'll all share."

Gaither used the story to illustrate the nature of God's love, and how He invites us to bring our small gifts and allow Him to multiply them through His bounty.

Maybe we should all adopt the policy of my niece's church, where shared dinners are a weekly occurrence. They have stopped calling such affairs "potluck" and instead, call them "pot-blessings."

2
Is that all?

"There's nothing to eat." My son stood in front of the refrigerator holding the door open, gazing forlornly into the interior.

"Don't be silly," I said. "There's plenty to eat in there."

He shook his head, closed the door and walked away. He began rummaging through the cupboards, opening and closing one door after another.

"What are you looking for?" I asked.

"I don't know. I just want something to eat."

I went to the refrigerator to have a look for myself. After all, it had been about two hours since I last looked in. The contents of a refrigerator can change a lot in two hours when there are kids in the house.

There was food in the refrigerator, just as I remembered, but I had to admit, the gaps in there made it look like a second-grader's gums.

"See?" my son said, looking over my shoulder. "I told you. There's nothing to eat."

It was payday morning. There was one egg, and about half a cup of milk in the bottom of a gallon container. There was no butter or margarine, except about three tablespoons on the plate by the toaster. The fruit juice had been finished off in an after-school raid a couple days before.

I took out the egg and milk. "I'll make pancakes for breakfast," I said.

"There isn't any syrup."

We ate pancakes with syrup made from brown sugar, water and maple flavoring. There were exactly two slices of bread to make one peanut butter sandwich for the brown bag lunch. I dropped the last apple into the bag, found a muffin in the freezer and called it dessert. I gave my son some change from the phone money jar to get a morning snack from the vending machine and sent him to school.

I had another look in the refrigerator, just in case something had spontaneously erupted in there while I had been occupied. The whole kitchen was pretty bleak. Oh, there were things like potatoes and onions and spaghetti, flour and sugar and cornmeal, corn flakes and Cream of Wheat, canned beans and corn and sliced mushrooms and soup, but there was nothing to eat, nothing quick and easy, nothing festive, nothing fun.

That's what most Americans mean when they say there's nothing to eat. They mean there are no juice boxes, no granola bars, no Little Debbie snack cakes, no cookies or fruit leather. There are no chips or cheese dip, no pre-cut celery and carrots, no bowls of leftover lasagna, meatloaf, pot roast or mashed potatoes. There's no processed sandwich meat and no frozen pizza.

Yes, resourceful cook that I am, I could have concocted several meals from the groceries on hand, but I was thankful that morning I didn't have to. My cupboards were bare because I'd been so busy working I hadn't had time to shop, a crisis of decidedly minor proportions. It reminded me, though, of families that wake up to such depressing kitchens day after day. They aren't starving, but they also aren't satisfied.

3
All I need is an apron

I was putting some icing on cupcakes the other day when it hit me. I had turned into a church lady.

I've heard about the "church lady" comedy routine developed by comedian Dana Carvey for the Saturday Night Live television show, but I never actually saw it. I don't know if I would have enjoyed it, since I know and appreciate so many of the real church ladies whose lives revolve around good works. Like anyone who is sincere and ingenuous, church ladies are easy prey for mockers and mimics. I can't fault Carvey, since I don't know his background, but in my experience, church ladies are often the first to laugh at their own idiosyncrasies.

What surprised me was that somewhere along the line, I became one of those ladies who had been the pillars of my life. Pearl and Yvonne and Corena and Violet, Marilyn and Reba and Fayona and Leah, Helen and Libby and Mary and Gertrude and Edith, and of course, my own mother, Blanche, were the ones we all counted on. Nothing had to be said. Of course they would come through with food for any occasions, be it wedding or funeral, Mother's Day lunch or church picnic, Christmas program popcorn balls or vacation Bible school brownies, youth group taffy pulls or work day potluck dinners or meals delivered to the homes of those who were sick or who had new babies.

They fed us in other ways, too. They were Sunday school teachers and nursery workers. They washed the communion set and folded the Sunday service bulletin. They were my examples just by being who they were. As long as I live I will remember the eyes of the church lady who had been my fifth-grade Sunday school teacher boring into me as I stood saying my wedding vows to my husband. I wouldn't dare break my word. My husband might forgive me, but she expected more.

Like the rest of the young people in my church, I didn't think about the church ladies. They were part of the furniture, like the pulpit and the coat rack. In those days it seemed impossible that I would become like them. They had weird hair styles and wore dresses that were too long to be fashionable and cried when they read poems at the church programs. If we thought of them at all, it was as extensions of our mothers – people whose greatest joy in life was to serve us.

For a lot of years, I thought the church ladies only existed in rural communities. I thought that if they had traveled or been to college they wouldn't have time or inclination for the menial tasks that needed doing in the church. When I hit the big city, I thought there would be trained professionals who would more efficiently and more elegantly perform the kind of work they had done.

    I was wrong. Church ladies are pretty much the same the world over, a tightly knit group of women who, under normal circumstances, may have little in common and may not even enjoy each other's company, but who rise to any occasion to nurture and comfort their own.

    The cupcakes I was icing were for a funeral lunch, for the comfort and convenience of those who would be coming to bid farewell to one of our deacons who had died after a lingering illness. Making the cupcakes, I thought of all those church ladies from my youth, some of them now also gone to glory.

    Now I'm the one making the Jell-O salad and the ground bologna sandwich spread. I can't say exactly how the transition from being served to serving took place, but as I put a little swirl on the vanilla frosting, I took satisfaction at having joined an elite group.

4
Measuring the memories

The other day I was struck with the urge to organize my recipes. I sat down with a cup of coffee, a stack of 3"X 5" index cards (children: ask your grandmother for a definition), three new pens, my ragged old cookbooks, and an avocado and green file box stuffed with scraps of paper, each bearing a recipe and odd bits of dried food.

This time, I'm really going to put this stuff in order, I silently pledged, and dumped everything onto the table. What a mess! *I am truly disgusted by such inefficiency.*

Here's an envelope with the end torn off printed with the return address of some mission organization I never heard of. Across the back is written, in old-school penmanship, the recipe for "Oatmeal Cake." I know where this came from. Marie, the camp cook, wrote it out for me one day as I looked at the glob of leftover hot cereal rejected by unhappy campers. She wrote it from memory, of course, talking as she wrote. I still see her Swedish blue eyes dancing and remember the joy she found in her work, her family and her faith.

Well, I'll just keep this as a memento, but the rest – something must be done. Look at all these recipes I've never even cooked, not even once! I'll just throw them out. Here's one called Korean Tuna Salad. Let's see, this came from my neighbor, Nancy. She gave it to me when she was still married, before that day when she and I stood in front of the courthouse elevator crying over the too-soon and too-simple end to her 11-year marriage. I'll keep this, a little picture of happier days, but this is the last one – except for Bev's mashed potato cake, and of course, Grannie Runyon's mirotan of beef, and Sherry VanKuiken's …who is Sherry VanKuiken, anyway?

I have far too many cookbooks. I'll just copy out the recipes I use – about one from each volume. But there are some cute cartoons in this one, some inspirational readings here, there a photo good enough for framing, if I ever get around to it. Here's this old recipe book my sister helped produce when her kids were in elementary school. The binder's gone, the pages are held in a bundle with a rubber band. It's so shabby from all these years of use. She was so proud of it, and I was proud of her for having helped create it. Even though her name appeared on only one recipe in the whole book, I envied her for having her name in print.

Oh well, books are easy to keep. Why copy what's already on the page? But this one, for sure, has to go. It's impossible to use. The edges are brown and tattered, the pages are stuck together because it has laid open on the countertop for so many hours while I pored over recipes, and in the process, poured recipes over it. This book taught me how to bake bread and cinnamon rolls, how to season tomatoes with dill and beef with cloves, how to create a Thanksgiving dinner for two with Cornish hens garnished with frosted grapes and how to stretch a pound of ground beef to feed five people. The cover is scorched and scratched, the original colors faded beyond recognition.

But this book was a wedding gift from my mother. She knew better than anyone that through all the unknowns encountered in building a life, good food would be a welcome and blessed invariable. I can't part with it.

The coffee's gone. The pens are still new. I bundle the collection of old grocery receipts, envelopes, candy bar wrappers, note paper, hunks of cardboard packaging, church bulletins and scraps of grocery bags back into the awful green and orange box, which was a gift from my secret pal in some long-forgotten diet club.

If I had time, I would really get down to sorting this stuff out, but today doesn't seem to be just right for cleaning out leftovers, especially not the leftover memories.

TABLE GRACE

Praying at mealtimes makes a lot of sense, partly because mealtimes happen regularly and often. The simplest, and in my opinion best table grace is this:
God is great, God is good.
Let us thank Him for our food.
All our anxiety in life comes from doubts in these two areas. Is God really great? Is He capable of handling the situation? Is He really good? If I trust Him, will He do something that will hurt me?
God is great – all-powerful, all knowing, everywhere present. He is good, the essence of love, without guile or spite or vengefulness. His provision of food is evidence of both. Thanking Him for it is an appropriate act of praise and builds faith within ourselves and our children.
(With deference to David Jenista, Sunday school teacher)

My "Connection Collection"
Recipes that Bridge the Miles & Years

Food is the most natural connection between humans. Eating together is a universal act of trust and camaraderie. In our culture, asking for the recipe is a compliment to the cook and a sign of humility in the one giving the request. "You gave me pleasure," the request says. "Show me how, so I may pass pleasure along to others."

The recipes in my collection remind me of those who gave them and of the meals where they were served – the Thanksgivings and Christmases spent with family, the funeral lunches where goodbyes were said, the birthday parties and graduations and weddings where hopes were expressed and bonds forged. They remind me of those who showed their love through hours in the kitchen, not cooking fancy food with expensive ingredients, but preserving food gleaned from the earth and trying to make something out of nothing for hungry kids who didn't understand economics.

While gathering recipes for this collection, I received this e-mail from a cousin, Lori Schonert: "Aunt Jean (Hulliberger) babysat us for a while when my mom worked at the bank. One of the good things about going to Aunt Jean's house was getting to eat these sweet, crunchy pickles. She knew I liked them and one year for Christmas gave me my very own jar of the 'green jewels!' They probably go by different names, depending on who you ask, but I have them as 'Society Sweet Pickles,'" (page 81). That shows the power of food to join us to loved ones through the years.

Here's a small sampling of recipes I have collected over the past 40 years, including, in some cases, a few personal remarks about the giver. I hope reading them, and perhaps cooking them, will help you experience times when the food is good, but love is the main dish being served.

DISCLAIMER: The recipes in this collection have been written by everyday cooks who assume the reader knows something about the kitchen – for instance, that you need to pre-heat the oven before putting a cake in to bake, the difference between dicing and mincing, and the difference between condensed and evaporated milk. Directions may be skimpy. If you have questions, ask a friend or an older relative. It's a great way to learn to cook, and to build relationships.

-- Thanks, Mom! --

Blanche Kenyon's
THREE-GRAIN BREAD

When I think of my mother, I often visualize her in the kitchen, kneading bread dough. She bought flour in 25-pound bags and baked bread at least weekly for many years, then graduated to less frequent but larger batches, making rolls for open houses and family parties. This is a recipe she began making when I was in high school.

STIR TOGETHER:
1 cup white flour
2 cups whole wheat flour
1 cup rolled oats
1/4 cup wheat germ
1/4 cup yellow corn meal
2 teaspoons salt
2 pkgs. dry yeast

COMBINE:
1 cup hot water
1/4 cup margarine
one 13-oz. can evaporated milk
1/4 cup honey
Add to flours, beat two minutes with mixer
Beat in 2 eggs

Gradually add 2 1/2 to 3 cups white flour, mixing by hand

Knead a few minutes. Let rise until double. Divide into two loaves and put in pans. Let loaves rise until double. Bake at 375 degrees for 20 minutes. Lower oven temperature to 350 degrees, bake 30 to 35 minutes.

Elsie Runyon's
APPLESAUCE WALNUT CAKE

Runyon, my husband's mother, knew how to feed her five children on [wi]dow's pension, but also appreciated fine food. Her first question when [she c]ame to visit was always, "Did you eat yet?"

[BLE]ND IN LARGE BOWL:
- 2 cups flour
- ? cups sugar
- [tea]spoon salt
- [tea]spoon nutmeg
- [tea]spoon ginger
- [tea]spoons cinnamon
- [tea]spoons cloves
- [tea]spoons baking soda

[BLEND] IN SEPARATE BOWL:
- butter (unsalted)
- [eg]gs
- [tea]spoons lemon extract
- [tea]spoons vanilla extract
- [cup]s chunky apple sauce
- [a]nd raisins
- chopped dates
- [cup]s walnuts, coarsely chopped.

[Mix a]ll ingredients with a spoon until well blended. Bake in loaf pans at 275 [degre]es for about two hours. When top begins to crack and the sides pull [away] from the pan, check the middle of the cake for doneness with a [tooth]pick.

[When] cool, if you want to keep the cakes for longer than two weeks, soak [sever]al layers of cheese cloth in brandy or rum and wrap the cakes like you [would] any good fruitcake and store in an airtight container. Mom said, for [best] results, use homemade applesauce and fresh, hand-cracked black [walnu]ts.

-- FROM THE SISTERS --

Pat Duimstra's
BEEF STEW

My sister Pat has always thrown herself totally into any endeavor, from being a high school drum majorette to having seven children to opening a restaurant with her husband when they were at retirement age. Cooking is no different. She does it with class, originality and energy. I got this recipe from her not long after I was married, and have used it ever since.

HEAT 2 tablespoons oil in large saucepan.
BROWN 2 to 3 pounds cubed stewing beef in the oil (chuck roast works)

ADD:
2 quarts hot water
1 large onion, sliced thin
1/4 teaspoon garlic powder or 1 clove minced garlic
1/3 teaspoon pepper
1/3 teaspoon paprika
1/4 teaspoon cloves
1 teaspoon sugar
1/2 teaspoon lemon juice
2 bay leaves

Cover, bring to boil, then reduce heat. Let simmer until meat is tender, about two hours. Add peeled, cubed potatoes and carrots as desired, usually four to six of each. Simmer until vegetables are tender. Thicken just before serving with about two tablespoons cornstarch softened in a little water.

Shirley Southern's
Baked Beans

Dinner with the family on Sunday afternoon has been a family tradition for Shirley and her husband, Moses, for many years. Southern-style dishes like green beans and ham and fried chicken and gravy were treats my own children looked forward to on visits to "Aunt Sis."

BROWN IN SKILLET:
1 pound hamburger; drain, set aside

FRY, then CHOP:
1/2 pound bacon

MIX:
3/4 cup brown sugar
3/4 cup ketchup
1 teaspoon dry mustard
2 tablespoons vinegar
1/2 medium onion, chopped; or 2 teaspoons onion powder
1 tablespoon salt
1/4 to 1/2 teaspoon black pepper
3 15-ounce cans pork and beans

Add meat and bake at 350 degrees for one hour.

Nancy Hatfield's
Everyday Meat Loaf

After Nancy married my brother, she followed him from one Air Force post to another for 10 years, presenting him with five children along the way. After the service, he went to Bible school and entered the ministry. She came along with him, growing in faith, always making do with little money. Simple, hearty meals were an expression of her love.

COMBINE:
2 eggs, beaten
3/4 cup milk

ADD:
1/2 cup fine breadcrumbs
1/3 cup chopped onion
2 teaspoons snipped fresh
   parsley, or dried parsley
1 teaspoon salt
1/2 teaspoon ground sage
1/8 teaspoon pepper

ADD TO EGG MIXTURE:
1 1/2 pound ground beef
1/2 pound pork sausage

Spoon mixture into ring mold or large bread pan. Bake at 350 degrees for 50 minutes. Remove pan from oven and drain liquid.
TOP WITH GLAZE:
1/2 c. ketchup
1 tablespoon brown sugar
1 teaspoon dried mustard

Put back in oven and bake 10 more minutes.

Susan River's
Vegetable Lasagne

As a young mother, my sister Sue made simple, wholesome food that was familiar and satisfying — comfort food. As a retiree, she fed the same kinds of meals to the senior citizen's group. She has given up meat and dairy products now, finding new satisfaction in cooking demonstrations for the StartNew program. Here is her version of vegetable lasagna.

Vegetable Sauce

STEAM OR MICROWAVE until tender:
2 large carrots, sliced
2 cups broccoli, bite-size pieces
Set aside.

COMBINE AND SAUTE in large skillet until tender:
1 tablespoon olive oil
2 thinly-sliced stalks celery
1 large red bell pepper, chopped
2 small zucchini, sliced or chopped
2 small yellow squash, sliced or chopped.

ADD:
4 green onions, sliced
4 to 6 cloves fresh garlic, minced
4 teaspoons dried basil
2 teaspoons dried oregano
1/2 teaspoon salt
Cook two minutes.

ADD:
8 cups diced fresh tomatoes, or canned tomatoes with one-third of juice drained
1 6-ounce can tomato paste
4 tablespoons lemon juice
4 tablespoons honey
cooked carrots and broccoli.

(continued on next page)

Herbed Tofu Mixture

Mash together until smooth:
1 pound tofu
2 tablespoons olive oil
1 tablespoon lemon juice
2 teaspoons honey
2 teaspoons garlic powder
1 teaspoon dried basil
1 teaspoon Italian seasoning

<u>To assemble:</u>
Cook an 18-ounce box of lasagna noodles eight to 10 minutes. Drain and lay out flat to cool slightly. Spray a three-inch-deep 9"x13" pan with baking spray. Put 3 cups vegetable/tomato sauce in pan. Top with half the noodles. Top noodles with 3 cups vegetable sauce. Spoon half of tofu mixture onto vegetable sauce in strips about three inches wide the length of the noodles. Repeat with another layer of noodles, vegetable sauce, and tofu mixture.

Bake 45 minutes at 350 degrees until top is slightly browned.

-- FROM THE AUNTS --

Society Sweet Pickles

14 medium cucumbers, washed

<u>1st day:</u>
Pour fresh, boiling water over whole cucumbers. For three more days, drain picked and repeat.

<u>5th day:</u>
Cut cucumbers in chunks.
Combine the following ingredients and pour over the chunks:
1 teaspoon salt
1 teaspoon pickling spices
6 to 8 cups sugar
1 quart. white vinegar

<u>6th day:</u>
Pour off liquid and bring it to a boil. Pour over pickles.

<u>7th day:</u>
Put cucumbers and spiced syrup into a pan and bring to a boil. Divide hot cucumber chunks and syrup evenly among glass pint jars. Add 1 1/2-teaspoon celery seed and a piece of cinnamon stick to each jar. Seal and process in boiling water bath.

Edith Bontekoe's
Sauerkraut Salad

MIX:
1 large can sauerkraut, drained and rinsed slightly
1/2 cup sweet red pepper, chopped fine
1/2 cup green bell pepper, chopped fine
1/2 cup sweet onion, chopped fine
2/3 cup celery, chopped fine

COMBINE and heat to boiling:
2 cups sugar
2/3 cup white vinegar
Cool and pour over vegetable mix. Chill. This keeps a long time in the refrigerator and taste improves with time.

Myrtle Joslin's
Molasses Cookies

Given to her by my geat-grandmother, Emily Joslin.

MIX
1 cup margarine (original recipe calls for lard)
1 cup sugar

ADD and MIX WELL:
1 cup molasses
1 cup cold water

DISSOLVE 3 teaspoons soda in 1/4 cup hot water. Add to above ingredients and mix.

BLEND and add to other ingredients:
1 1/2 tsp. ginger
1 teaspoon cinnamon
1 teaspoon baking powder
6 cups flour

Pour dough out onto heavily floured board. Knead in enough flour to make dough stiff enough to handle. Divide into fourths and roll to quarter-inch thick. Sprinkle with white sugar and pat into dough. Cut in circles and bake on ungreased cookie sheet. Repeat with rest of dough. Re-roll leftover dough and cut, but avoid adding more flour.

Leah Wilson's
Pumpkin Torte

MIX:
24 crushed graham crackers
1/3 cup sugar
1/2 cup butter or margarine, melted
Press into a 9" x 13" pan.

MIX:
2 beaten eggs
3/4 cup sugar
8-ounce pkg. cream cheese

Pour over crust and bake 20 minutes at 350 degrees. Cool.

MIX:
2 cups canned pumpkin
3 egg yolks
1/2 cup sugar
1/2 cup milk
1/2 teaspoon salt
1 tablespoon cinnamon

Cook over medium heat until mixture thickens. Remove from heat and add:
1 envelope unflavored gelatin dissolved in 1/4 cup cold water. Cool.

BEAT UNTIL STIFF:
3 egg whites
1/4 cup sugar

Fold into pumpkin mixture. Pour mixture over baked, cooled crust. Top with whipped cream. Makes 24 generous servings.

Cindy Joslin's
Sugar Cookies

CREAM:
2 cups butter or margarine
1 teaspoon vanilla
1 1/2 cups sugar
3 eggs, beating well after each addition

BLEND:
3 1/2 cups sifted all-purpose flour
2 teaspoons cream of tartar
2 teaspoons soda
1/2 teaspoon salt
Mix with wet ingredients. Chill three to four hours.

Roll dough to 1/8- to 1/4-inch thick on well-floured surface and cut in desired shapes. Bake on ungreased cookie sheet at 375 degrees for six to eight minutes. Cool slightly on cookie sheet, then finish on racks. Decorate as you like.

Jean Hulliberger's
Rabbit Casserole

Cut one cleaned rabbit into pieces. Par-boil rabbit in water with a little vinegar. Skim foam as the meat cooks. Boil until tender. Cool slightly and remove meat from bones.

MIX:
4 oz. sour cream
1 can cream of celery soup
Add rabbit and put mixture in baking dish.

Prepare one box Stovetop stuffing mix according to directions. Spoon stuffing onto rabbit mixture. Bake at 350 degrees a half-hour. (This is good made with chicken, too.)

Helen Joslin's
Herb-Celery Turkey Dressing

1 pound white bread
1/2 cup diced onion
1 1/4 cups diced celery
3/4 cup butter or margarine
1/8 teaspoon salt
1/4 teaspoon pepper
1/2 teaspoon poultry seasoning
1 1/2 teaspoon sage
Broth or hot water as desired to moisten

FREEZE a one-pound loaf of white bread.
Cut the frozen slices into small cubes, or coarsely grate the bread.

Saute celery and onion in butter until tender, but not brown. Add sautéed vegetables and seasonings to bread crumbs. Mix well. Turn into a greased 1 1/2 quart baking dish. Bake at 350 degrees for 45 minutes. Yield: 1 1/2 quarts dressing.

Ruth Dalton's
Banana Spice Cake

MIX:
2 1/2 cups sifted flour
2 1/2 teaspoons baking powder
1/2 teaspoon soda
3/4 teaspoon salt
1/8 teaspoon cloves (optional)
1 1/4 teaspoon cinnamon
1/2 teaspoon nutmeg
Set aside.

CREAM:
1/2 cup solid shortening
1 1/4 cup sugar

ADD:
2 eggs beating well after each addition
1 teaspoon vanilla

ADD:
1 1/2 cups mashed bananas (three medium and one large), alternating with flour mixture.
Bake in 9"x13" pan at 350 degrees about 30 minutes, or an 8-inch square pan and 10 cupcakes.

Note: oil may be substituted for the shortening.

-- FROM FRIENDS --

I've been blessed with many friends. Some have interacted with me on some level for as many as 40 or 50 years. This section could contain hundreds of entries. These few represent friendship at many levels of duration and sharing.

Beth Elve's
Brunch Enchiladas

Beth Elve was a friend from church who died in early middle-age from a brain tumor. Her no-nonsense faith was evidenced in her service to the church, generous hospitality, and her relentless love for her husband and daughters, one of whom was severely disabled.

Brown in skillet:
1 pound bulk breakfast sausage
1/4 cup chopped green onion
1/4 cup chopper green pepper

Add:
2 cups grated Cheddar or Colby cheese

Divide meat and cheese mixture evenly among eight 8-inch flour tortillas, about 1/2 cup each. Roll tortillas, leaving ends open. Arrange seam-side down in greased 9"x13" baking dish.

Mix:
4 eggs
2 cups milk
1 tablespoon flour
1/8 teaspoon garlic powder.

Pour egg mixture over tortillas. Cover with foil and refrigerate overnight. Bake covered at 350 degrees for 45 to 50 minutes. Remove cover, top with 2 cups grated cheese and bake five minutes. Let stand 10 minutes before serving.

Marian Stevens'
Fresh Peach Cake

One of those highly efficient and seemingly tireless people, Marian wrote a recipe page for the Advance Newspaper for many years and produced her own cookbook, "Mealtime at Marian's." This is from her collection.

2 1/2 cups fresh peaches, crushed
2 eggs
2 cups flour
2 cups sugar
2 teaspoons baking soda
1/2 teaspoon salt

Crush peeled peaches, using potato masher or food processor. In large mixing bowl, beat eggs until light. Add crushed peaches. Blend dry ingredients and add to peaches and eggs. Spread batter in a greased and floured 9"x13" pan. Bake at 350 degrees for 30 to 40 minutes, or until cake tests done.

Put topping on cake as soon as it comes from the oven.
TOPPING:
1/2 cup margarine
1 small (5-ounce) can evaporated milk
3/4 cup sugar
1 teaspoon vanilla
1 cup flaked coconut
1 cup chopped nutmeats.
Melt margarine in medium-sized saucepan. Stir in milk and sugar. Bring mixture to a boil and cook for two minutes. Remove from heat and stir in vanilla, coconut and nutmeats. Spread over hot cake.

Bev Mullens'
Broccoli Rice Casserole

Bev was my college roommate, and despite long lapses in communication (we share the blame), has remained a cherished friend throughout my life. She has overcome many enemies, both physical and spiritual. I am indebted to her not only for her enduring faithfulness, but because she introduced me to my husband.

COOK:
1/2 cup rice in 1 cup water

COOK:
two 10-ounce packages chopped, frozen broccoli
(or about four cups fresh broccoli)

SAUTE UNTIL TENDER:
1/2 cup chopped onion
1/2 cup chopped celery
4 tablespoons butter

MIX:
all vegetables and rice

ADD:
one 10.5-oz. can cream of mushroom soup
one 8-ounce jar Cheeze Whiz with jalapeno pepper

Pour into casserole dish and bake at 350 degrees until bubbly.

Sharon Miller's
Baby Back Ribs

I met Sharon when I was asked by a publisher to read the manuscript for a new book she had written. She became one of the greatest influencers of my writing career, and continues to be my friend.

Line a baking pan with foil, leaving extra to completely cover the contents. Put pork ribs in the pan, and spread with Sweet Baby Ray's barbecue and rib sauce. Fold foil and seal. Refrigerate for 24 hours. Bake in foil at 250 degrees for 4 to 5 hours.

Nancy Sheets'
Pineapple Green Jell-O

At first a neighbor, then a friend, Nancy has blessed me with her ingenuousness, her classiness, and her humility and submission before God as He led her through deep waters.

6-ounce pkg. lime gelatin
8-ounce pkg. cream cheese
3/4 cup miniature marshmallows
15-ounce can crushed pineapple

Drain pineapple, reserving juice. Mix juice with enough water to make two cups. Prepare gelatin according to directions, using juice and water mixture for the cold water measure. Refrigerate gelatin until slightly firm.

Beat cream cheese until soft. Whip gelatin, and blend into cream cheese. Add drained pineapple and marshmallows. Pour into a 9"x13 pan and refrigerate until firm.

--A CHRISTMAS COLLECTION--

I love making cookies, breads and candy to give away as gifts during the Christmas season, but there are conditions. First, I don't give sweets to people who don't want them – those who have diet restrictions or who by choice don't eat refined sugar. Second, I give only a few, well-chosen cookies, preferably at a time when I can enjoy then with the recipient (If we are talking about a college dormitory or church youth group, however, these suggestions do not apply. More is always better.)

I like the selections in this sampling because of their ease of preparation and diversity in color, texture and flavor. There must be at least a million Christmas cookie and candy recipes, with more every year, but these are tried and true, not too fancy, old-fashioned kinds of treats with special holiday touches.

Chex Party Mix

The recipe is on the cereal box, but I like to substitute tiny pretzels and goldfish crackers for some of the dry ingredients, and add more nuts. Make double batches and store in plastic bags just big enough to hold one cup. These make great gifts for co-workers, especially those who don't appreciate candy or other sweets.

Holiday Raspberry Gelatin Salad

HEAT: 1 c. water to boiling
ADD: 4 tablespoons hot cinnamon candy. Stir until dissolved. Reheat candy and water to boiling, and stir in 1 box (four-serving size) raspberry gelatin, regular or sugar-free. Stir until dissolved.

ADD: 1 cup applesauce
Pour into 8 parfait glasses and cool. Top each serving with whipped topping and a mint leaf, or cool in an 8"x8" glass pan and cut into eight servings.

Church Windows

Miniature marshmallows surrounded by chocolate give the appearance of leaded stained glass windows – well, with a little imagination, anyway.

MELT TOGETHER:
12-ounce package dark (semi-sweet) chocolate chips
1/2 cup butter or margarine.

STIR IN:
10 1/2-ounce package colored miniature marshmallows
1 cup chopped walnuts.
Stir until marshmallows are well coated.

On a sheet of aluminum foil, put 1cup shredded coconut in a narrow row. Drop chocolate mixture by large spoonfuls onto coconut to make a roll, using about 1/3 of the mixture. Move chocolate roll back and forth to coat completely with coconut, then seal in the foil and refrigerate. Repeat to make two more rolls. When needed, slice rolls. Slice when ready to use.

Millie Bamford's
Eggnog

I never met Millie, but her son, Paul, worked with my husband for a while. Paul brought this delightfully rich eggnog to a birthday party we managed to spring on my husband, one of two really good surprise parties in his life. None of those who were guests are still involved in our life, yet the memory of the day lives on through this recipe. Such is the power of food and friendship.

MIX:
2 well-beaten eggs
one 15-oz. can sweetened condensed milk
1 teaspoon vanilla
1/4 teaspoon salt

ADD:
1 quart whole milk

Chill milk-egg mixture. When ready to serve, whip 1/2-pint heavy cream and fold into mixture. Top with nutmeg, if desired.

Glenda Brown's
New Year's Day Chili Dog Topping

Glenda Brown filled me in on all the local gossip on my first beat as a reporter for the Advance Newspaper. Chili dogs were a New Year's Day tradition at her house even before TV bowl games became popular.

COMBINE in saucepan:
2 cups cold water
1 pound ground beef
1 small can tomato paste
1 small onion, chopped fine
2 tablespoons paprika
1 tablespoon chili powder

Heat gradually to boiling, stirring occasionally. Reduce heat, simmer uncovered 90 minutes.

FOR GREAT FAMILY-STYLE CHILI:
Make as directed, then add a 14-oz. can chili beans, 1 quart (32 ounces) canned tomatoes, extra salt and pepper to taste.

Refrigerator Fruitcake

A cross between pecan log and date bars, this recipe is colorful, easy to make and keeps well. Slice when needed. Remember, some people DO like fruitcake, and this is an easy way to give the traditional treat in moderation.

MELT TOGETHER:
1 1/2 sticks butter or margarine
1/2 pound marshmallows

STIR IN:
2 tablespoons brown sugar
1 teaspoon vanilla
1 cup graham cracker crumbs
1/2 pound pecan halves
1 pound pitted dates, chopped
1/4 pound candied cherries
1/8 pound candied citron or mixed fruit
1/3 pound candied pineapple, chopped

Mix well. Form into rolls and wrap first in waxed paper, then aluminum foil, or press into loaf pans, and store in refrigerator. Slice when ready to serve.

--CHRISTMAS (OR ANY TIME) COOKIES --

Snow Drop Sugar Cookies

This recipe came to me from a friend, Carol Sterken, who once told me she feared that when she was dead, she would leave behind nothing of importance. Wrong! Not only did she raise three sons, she passed along this recipe.

CREAM TOGETHER:
1/2 cup powdered sugar
1/2 cup granulated sugar
1/2 cup butter
1/2 cup vegetable oil
1 egg

ADD:
2 cups plus 1 1/2 teaspoons flour
1/8 teaspoon salt
1/2 teaspoon soda
1/2 teaspoon cream of tartar
1/2 teaspoon vanilla

Drop by spoonfuls onto parchment-lined baking sheet. Bake 12 to15 minutes at 325 degrees. These cookies are white, and look nice decorated with half a maraschino cherry, candied red or green cherry, or colored sprinkles.

Ginger Crinkles

I first encountered these cookies when I walked into Nancy Furhman's house on a winter evening. The house was filled with the wonderful aroma of spices and molasses. She gave me this recipe, which has become a family favorite all year 'round. Don't over-bake, and they will be soft and chewy.

CREAM:
3/4 cup margarine
1 cup sugar
ADD:
1/4 cup dark molasses
1 egg

(continued on next page)

ADD:
2 cups flour
1/4 teaspoon salt
1 teaspoon cloves
1 teaspoon ginger
1 teaspoon cinnamon
1/2 teaspoon soda

Shape dough into balls about the size of a walnut, then roll them in sugar, Bake at 375 degrees about 10 minutes, just until cracks appear. Allow cookies to cool slightly before removing from baking sheet.

Good News Camp Cocoa Brownies

My yeas on staff at Good News Camp (Gladwin, Mich.) was my introduction to cooking for large groups. This simple recipe is a good one to fill the chocolate spot on the cookie plate.

COMBINE in any order:
2 1/4 cups flour
3 cups sugar
3/4 teaspoon salt
3/4 cup baking cocoa
1 1/2 cups softened margarine
6 eggs
3 teaspoons vanilla
1 1/2 cups chopped nuts.

Beat with mixer until smooth. Bake at 325 degrees about 25 minutes in a 9"x13" pan. Add icing, if you like, or dust with powdered sugar.

Classic Peanut Butter Cookies

I like this recipe because there's only one fraction, and that ingredient is optional. It's from the mother's club cookbook given to me by my sister, Pat Duimstra, the first year I was married. Try it with almond butter or cashew butter if you are giving them to someone with peanut allergy.

CREAM:
2 cup shortening
1 cup brown sugar
1 cup white sugar

ADD and MIX:
1 cup peanut butter
2 eggs
1 teaspoon vanilla

ADD and MIX:
1 teaspoon baking soda
1 teaspoon baking powder
3 cups flour
1/4 teaspoon salt (if using natural peanut butter)

Pack dough into small bread tins and cool overnight. Slice and bake 15 minutes at 350 degrees.

Emergency Peanut Butter Cookies

Just three ingredients!

MIX:
1 cup peanut butter
1 cup sugar
1 egg

Mix until texture changes and dough appears slightly dryer. Drop dough by tablespoons onto baking sheet. Flatten slightly with fork. Bake at 350 degrees for about 10 minutes. Let cool before removing from pan. Makes 18 small cookies.

Mincemeat Cookies

One of the few cookies my husband really likes – spicy, soft, cake-like cookies that freeze well, if put in layers separated by waxed paper.

CREAM:
1 cup butter or margarine or shortening
1 1/2 cups white sugar
3 eggs

ADD:
2 cups prepared mincemeat
3 1/4 cup sifted flour
1 teaspoon baking powder
1 teaspoon soda
1/3 teaspoon salt
1 teaspoon ground allspice
1 teaspoon vanilla
1 cup chopped nuts

Drop dough by tablespoons on greased baking sheet. Bake at 375 degrees about 15 minutes. If you make your own mincemeat, you may want to reduce the amount of spices in the cookies.

Dream Cheesecakes

Little cheesecake bites that take a while to make, but make great gifts.

FILLING:
3 8-ounce packages cream cheese
1/2 teaspoon vanilla
1 cup sugar
5 eggs

TOPPING:
1 pint sour cream
1/4 cup sugar
1 teaspoon vanilla

Line cupcake pans with cupcake papers. Spoon about one tablespoon of filling into each cup. Bake at 350 degrees for 20 minutes, until top cracks slightly. Remove from oven and spoon small amount of topping onto each cake. Bake five minutes. Cool on racks. When cool, top with red or green candied cherry or dab of canned fruit pie filling.

NOTE: To make bite-size cheesecakes, use mini-muffin or candy papers available from cake decorating shops. Put them in mini-muffin pans, with a vanilla wafer in the bottom of each one, or a teaspoon of graham cracker pie crust mixture (recipe on graham cracker crumb box). Fill 2/3 with filling, and bake about 8-10 minutes, then add topping and bake 4 to 5 minutes. Decorate when cool. These are more time consuming, but are really cute and fun to eat.

Heath Bars

Linda Markham, a friend from church, gave me this recipe. Se has a gift for hospitality and hosted our cookie exchange for several years .This confection is very rich, and really is a lot like a Heath candy bar.

36 saltine crackers
1 cup brown sugar
1/2 pound real butter (no substitutes)
1 cup chopped nuts

Grease jelly-roll-size baking sheet that has sides. Place crackers on pan in a single layer.

Melt butter and sugar together in medium-sized saucepan. Bring to a boil over medium heat, and boil for three minutes, stirring occasionally.

Put baking sheet with crackers onto oven rack, then pour syrup over crackers. Bake five minutes at 400 degrees. Cook a few minutes, then sprinkle chocolate chips on top. Spread the chocolate when melted. Sprinkle nuts on top. Allow to cool completely before cutting.

Heirloom Plum Pudding

This is an old English recipe handed down from my great-grandmother. Who but the resourceful English could take sour milk and beef suet and make something so tantalizing?

MIX IN LARGE BOWL:
1 cup sugar
1 cup suet, ground fine

COAT WITH A LITTLE FLOUR:
2 cups raisins
1 cup mixed candied or other dried fruit (currants are a traditional add-in). Add to sugar and suet.

IN SEPARATE BOWL, MIX:
1 cup sour milk or buttermilk
1 teaspoon soda
3 tablespoons molasses
2 teaspoons vanilla

Mix dry and wet ingredients. Dough will be quite stiff. Sprinkle a large cotton cloth or flour sack with flour and put dough in center. Draw edges of cloth up around dough and tie loosely with string. Suspend bundle of dough in a pot of boiling water, or let rest on a rack. Steam for about an hour and a half. Let cool before loosening cloth.

SAUCE:
MIX:
1 1/2 tablespoon cornstarch
1/2 cup sugar
1/4 teaspoon vanilla
1 cup water
2 tablespoons vinegar
Cook until thick and clear; add 2 tablespoons water. Spoon onto slices of warm plumb pudding.

-- A FEW OFFERINGS OF MY OWN --

Potato Salad

It was a shock to me when a friend asked for my recipe for potato salad. I didn't know recipes for potato salad existed. I thought everyone made it with a spoonful of this and a spoonful of that, just like I did. I decided to write down the recipe, but I don't actually follow it. It's the idea that counts.

4 cups diced white potatoes (about 8 large, or 3 pounds)
6 eggs
1 cup diced celery
1/2 cup diced mild onions
1 1/4 cups real mayonnaise
2 tablespoons salad mustard
3 tablespoons sweet pickle relish
2 tablespoons sugar
1 tablespoon vinegar
1/2 teaspoon Lawry's seasoned salt

Boil eggs; cool, peel and chop.
Boil potatoes in jackets; cool slightly, peel and dice. Mix potatoes, eggs, celery and onions in large bowl.

Mix mayonnaise, mustard, relish, vinegar, sugar and seasoned salt. Pour over other ingredients and mix until blended. Garnish with parsley around edge, or cut boiled egg lengthwise into sections to make a daisy.

Triple Apple Dumplings

Great breakfast recipe, or quick stove-top dessert.
Low in refined sugar

Pour 4 cups apple cider into a 10" flat-bottom skillet with high sides, or other wide, flat saucepan.

Peel and finely chop:
1 medium to large peeled apple (about 1 cup)

Mix:
1 cup complete pancake mix
1/4 teaspoon cinnamon
1/8 teaspoon ground cloves
Dash nutmeg
1/3 cup unsweetened applesauce
1/2 cup apple cider

Add:
chopped apple and stir to blend

Bring cider to a gentle but constant boil. (Mulled cider increases flavor.) Drop apple batter into boiling cider using about two tablespoons per dumpling. Allow cider to return to boil. Cover and cook five minutes. Cider will thicken as dumplings plump. To serve, spoon thickened cider sauce over dumplings. Top with milk, thick cream, or whipped topping if desired.

Chowder Breakfast Muffins

1 pound sliced bacon
1/4 cup bacon drippings
1/2 cup diced onion
1 10 1/2-ounce can condensed cream of potato soup
1 1/4 c. milk
2 eggs
2 cups frozen white corn
1 1/2 cup self-rising white corn meal mix
1 tablespoon sugar
1 teaspoon baking powder
8 oz. shredded cheddar cheese

Dice uncooked bacon by cutting across stacked slices at 1/2-inch intervals. Fry until pieces until crisp. Remove bacon from drippings with a slotted spoon or spatula and drain on paper towels. Reserve 1/4 cup drippings. Pour remaining drippings from skillet except for about two teaspoons. Lightly sauté diced onion in remaining drippings in skillet.

In medium mixing bowl blend eggs, milk, and soup. Add frozen, uncooked corn. Blend corn meal mix, sugar and baking power and add to milk mixture. Add cooked bacon, sautéed onion and 1/4 c. bacon drippings. Blend mixture with large mixing spoon.

Spray jumbo muffin cups with non-stick spray or line with paper liners. Put about 3/4 cup muffin batter into each cup. Top each muffin with 2 tablespoons shredded cheddar cheese. Bake at 375 degrees for 30 to 35 minutes. Cool slightly before removing muffins from pans. Makes 8 jumbo muffins. (If making smaller muffins, reduce baking time to 25 min.) Flavor improves as muffins cool. One large one with a glass of juice makes a good breakfast for a working man.

Buttermilk Biscuits

MIX IN A FLAT-BOTTOM BOWL:
2 cups self-rising flour
1/8 teaspoon baking soda
2 teaspoons sugar

CUT IN UNTIL PARTICLES ARE FINE:
5 Tablespoons stick margarine

ADD GRADUALLY:
scant 1 cup buttermilk

Mix with fork until all flour mixture is moistened Dump onto floured surface, knead lightly three or four strokes. Pat dough out into a circle, about an inch thick, and cut with round cutter (drinking glass or soup can with ends but out works well.) Push extra pieces together and cut last biscuit, or pat into round shape. Place on shiny baking sheet with no sides, with biscuits just touching. Bake at 450 degrees just until tinged with brown, about 8 to 10 minutes. Eat piping hot with homemade strawberry jam.

TECHNIQUES GUARANTEED TO RUIN BISCUITS:
- Too much handling of the dough. Treat it gently.
- Too little milk. Dough should be moist, about like cooled oatmeal
- Too long in the oven. Take out as soon as tops are barely tinged golden brown.
- Baking too far in advance. Biscuits should be eaten hot out of the oven.

Chinese Chicken Casserole

This is one of the first recipes I tried after I got married. It is from the Pillsbury Family Cookbook, a wedding gift from my mother, modified to accommodate new ingredients.

COOK:
1 cup chopped celery in a little water until tender; drain

COMBINE:
Cooked celery
1 can condensed cream of mushroom soup
1 can cream of chicken soup
5-oz. can evaporated milk
3 cups chow mein noodles
1 1/2 cups cubed cooked chicken
4 ounce jar mushroom slices with liquid
1/2 cup toasted slivered almonds
1/2 cup chopped green pepper
1/2 cup chopped pimiento

Bake in a 9"x13" casserole dish at 350 degrees for one hour.

TAKING A MEAL TO SOMEONE? All the ingredients in this casserole can be purchased at the grocery store in cans or jars of approximately the right measure (except celery and green pepper) and taken in a bag or box to someone who needs help with meals. At his or her convenience, the person can open all the containers, combine and bake. Diced water-chestnuts can provide the crunch of the celery.

-- THINGS TO MAKE with HOME-CANNED TOMATOES --

Bachelor Spaghetti
Spaghetti in a single pan!

BROWN IN LARGE SKILLET:
1/2 pound hamburger or Italian sausage
1/2 large onion, chopped
1/2 fresh green pepper, chopped
4 ounces fresh mushrooms, sliced

ADD:
1 quart home-canned tomatoes with juice. Break up chunks
4 ounces dry spaghetti, broken roughly into quarters
2 teaspoons Italian spice mix
1/4 cup grated Parmesan cheese

Simmer, covered, until spaghetti is tender, about a half-hour. The cheese, and starch in the pasta, will thicken the sauce.

Easy All-vegetable Soup

COMBINE in large saucepan:
1 15-ounce can beef broth or vegetable broth
1 quart home-canned tomatoes and juice
1 can whole-kernel corn with juice
1 can peas with juice
1 can green beans with juice
1 can potatoes, sliced, with juice
1 can sliced carrots
1 medium onion, diced
2 celery ribs, diced
1 cup chopped cabbage, if you like it

Bring all to boil, reduce heat and simmer until celery and cabbage are tender.

Goulash
or something like it

COOK:
3 cups elbow macaroni in boiling water until tender, about 20 minutes (check package directions). Drain.

BROWN IN LARGE SKILLET:
1/2 pound ground beef
1 cup diced celery
1 medium onion, diced
1 medium green pepper, chopped, if you like it

ADD:
1 quart home-canned tomatoes with juice
cooked macaroni
1/2 teaspoon dill weed
1 can cream of tomato soup, undiluted
Simmer about 20 minutes.

Spanish Rice

COOK:
1/2 cup rice in 1 cup water.

BROWN IN LARGE SKILLET:
1/2 pound ground beef
1 cup diced celery
1 medium onion, diced
1 medium green pepper, chopped, if you like it

ADD:
1 quart home canned tomatoes with juice
cooked rice

Simmer 20 minutes or until tomato juice is mostly absorbed.

Randy Runyon's
Locally Famous Jambalaya

HAVE READY:
1 cup chicken stock
2 quarts tomatoes
8 ounces raw turkey or chicken breast in julienne strips
8 ounces of any one: turkey tasso, pork tasso or any good smoked pork or turkey, chopped into large pieces
4 links andouille sausage cut into 1/4-inch rounds (about 2 cups)

COMBINE in a small bowl:
1 tablespoon sweet paprika
1 tablespoon onion powder
1 tablespoon salt
2 teaspoons garlic powder
1 teaspoon white pepper
1 teaspoon black pepper
1 teaspoon dry mustard
1 teaspoon ground cumin
1/3 teaspoon cayenne pepper

CHOP into large pieces:
3 cups onion
3 cups green bell pepper
1 cup celery

Preheat a heavy five-quart pot, preferably nonstick, over high heat, about four minutes. Put in 2 cups, onion, 2 cups bell pepper, celery, tasso or smoked meat or poultry, 1 cup sausage, 3 tablespoons seasoning mix, and 3 bay leaves. Cook, scraping the bottom of the pot frequently, until the crust seems about to burn, about 12 minutes.

STIR IN Chicken broth.
Scrape the bottom of the pot to loosen all browned bits. Cook 10 minutes. Add the tomatoes, raw poultry, and remaining seasoning mix and cook five minutes. Add the remaining onions, peppers, andouille and stock and bring to a boil. Reduce heat to a slow simmer, cover and cook about 15 minutes.

Serve over hot cooked rice. (Some prefer to have three cups uncooked white rice added to the jambayala, plus 5 more cups chicken stock, and simmer until juice is absorbed and rice is tender.) SHRIMP may also be added. Cook five minutes.
*<u>Tasso ham and turkey are available at specialty stores, or substitute smoked turkey or country-style smoked ham.</u>

INDEX of RECIPES

Beverages
Eggnog, p. 92

Breads
Biscuits, buttermilk, p. 105
Bread, three grain, p. 74
Muffins, chowder breakfast, p. 104

Cakes
Applesauce walnut, p. 75
Banana spice, p. 86
Fresh peach, p. 88
Fruitcake, refrigerator, p. 94

Cookies and other Sweets
Brownies, p. 96
Church windows, p. 92
Ginger crinkles, p. 95
Heath bars, p. 100
Mincemeat cookies, p. 98
Molasses cookies, p. 82
Peanut butter cookies, classic, p. 97
Peanut butter cookies, emergency, p. 97
Plum pudding, heirloom, p. 101
Sugar cookies, Christmas, p. 84
Sugar cookies, snowdrop, p. 95

Desserts
Apple dumplings, triple, p. 103
Cheesecakes, p. 99
Pumpkin torte, p. 83

Main Dishes and Soup
Beef Stew, p. 76
Broccoli rice casserole, p. 89
Chicken, Chinese casserole, p. 106
Chili dog topping, p. 93
Chili, family style, p. 93
Enchiladas, brunch, p. 87
Goulash, p. 108
Jambalaya, p. 109
Lasagne, Vegetable, p. 79
Meat loaf, p. 78
Rabbit casserole, p. 84
Ribs, baby back, barbecued, p. 90
Soup, easy all vegetable, p. 107
Spaghetti, bachelor, p. 107
Spanish Rice, p. 108

Side Dishes and Salads
Beans, baked, p. 77
Dressing, herb-celery, p. 85
Pickles, sweet, p. 81
Pineapple green Jell-O, p. 80
Potato salad, p. 102
Sauerkraut Salad, p. 81
Raspberry gelatin, holiday, p. 91